THE GEORGIAN POETIC

THE GEORGIAN POETIC

By

Myron Simon

"Imagination's measureless towerings
Bear down upon the beds of reality"

—Gordon Bottomley

University of California Press
Berkeley • *Los Angeles* • *London*

UNIVERSITY OF CALIFORNIA PUBLICATIONS:
OCCASIONAL PAPERS

Number 8: Literature

University of California Press
Berkeley and Los Angeles
California

University of California Press, Ltd.
London, England

FOR AUSTIN WARREN

whose life is a miracle, which to relate
were not a history but a piece of poetry

PREFACE

In the address "To Criticize the Critic" (1961), T. S. Eliot acknowledged that in his early reaction against Georgian poetry and criticism he was "implicitly defending the sort of poetry" he and his friends wrote. Eliot's fine discrimination of personal motive illuminates a general motive in that debate between Georgian and Modernist, for much of the disapproving commentary on the Georgians is attributable to critics who were really advocating another kind of poetry. For example, Day Lewis's contemptuous dismissal of the Georgians as poets of "very low vitality" was surely a function of his revolutionary enthusiasm in 1934. His caricature of the Georgians, in *A Hope for Poetry*, served as a kind of rhetorical foil in an argument for the emergence of a genuinely revolutionary poetry. And throughout the twenties, thirties, and forties, critics engaged in promoting the successive waves of "new" poetry fastened on the Georgians as their premier instance of outmoded poetry. In the excitement of advocacy, they were scarcely disposed to look closely at the objects of their contempt, the "quaintly archaic" Georgians.

What was many times repeated assumed the appearance of an axiom, and thus passed into literary history. At last it was unnecessary even to read the Georgians in order to rehearse the charges against them, for the case presumably had already been made. The Georgians were so flattened out into the notorious counterexample of Modernist polemics that even the distinction between Edward Marsh's early Georgian circle and John Squire's Neo-Georgians was gradually lost.

And so the matter rested until the fifties, when full biographies, new editions, and the correspondence of the principal Georgians began to find their way into print, together with the first detailed history of *Georgian Poetry*. Taken together, these books demonstrate the unreliability of the early commentary on the Georgians; and they reveal the important contribution of the Georgians to the formation of twentieth-century English poetics. The historical scholarship of Christopher Hassall and Robert H. Ross is the point d'appui on which all future study of the Georgians must attempt to build, and my indebtedness to their work is very great indeed. I have sought to make good that debt by bringing some of the features on their map of the Georgians into sharper relief and by venturing to add some details.

Beyond the possibility of discharge are the obligations I owe to Austin Warren, my teacher and friend for twenty-five years. I am also permanently grateful to Harvey and Virginia Gross and to Herbert Howarth for their timely encouragements and friendship. I am indebted to Donald Hill, Emerson Marks, and Robert H. Ross for close readings of my manuscript. The New York Public Library has kindly granted me permission to quote from the letters of Edward Marsh in the Berg Collection.

M. S.

CONTENTS

1

THE REPUTATION OF
GEORGIAN POETRY

> For some years the collective reputation of the Georgians has
> been at a low ebb. Indeed, perhaps no group of poets since the
> Pre-Raphaelites has suffered more, or more ignominiously, from
> the widespread acceptance of oversimplified stereotypes and criti-
> cal half-truths, even among readers who should know better.
> Often the Georgians have been misrepresented because of the
> ignorance of their subsequent critics, but even more often they
> have been the victims of pure critical spleen.[1]

Any reader of the commentary on the Georgian poets is likely to
observe its sameness. Virtually all the witnesses concur in their
reports, and their testimony seems overwhelming in its conclusive-
ness. But, to carry the metaphor further, it is somehow disturbing
that so many different witnesses should provide so nearly identical
an account. Of course, the similarity of the testimony may be the
indisputable sign of its truth, but it may also suggest that the
witnesses have been coached. It may be that critics have been
disposed to view the Georgians "through spectacles provided . . .
by the later, more vigorous movement led by Pound and Eliot."[2]

For the past fifty years, the Georgians have been invoked
chiefly for purposes of deprecation; comparisons of them to other
spokesmen for contemporary poetry have been predictably invidi-
ous. Clearly, the designation "Georgian" has been pejorative. The
term connotes remoteness from the characteristic features of
twentieth-century life and conformity to exhausted traditions.
This connotation is fully implicit in the description of Georgian
poets as players upon "oaten pipes."[3] In her review of *Georgian*

1. Robert H. Ross, *The Georgian Revolt, 1910-1922* (Carbondale, Ill., 1965), p. ix.
2. C. K. Stead, The New Poetic (London, 1964), p. 81.
3. Louise Bogan, *Selected Criticism* (New York, 1955), p. 52.

[1]

Poetry: 1918-1919, Harriet Monroe made the point more explicitly:

> The "Georgians" live in the twentieth century, no doubt, but their subjects, ideals and methods follow the old standards of English song. . . . almost nothing in the book reminds us of the age we live in.[4]

For many years, the same charge has been commonly echoed. As John H. Johnston puts it, "The Georgian orientation toward the past was symptomatic of a general nostalgia; the gifted young men of the period all seemed intent on savoring the present as a golden, euphoric culmination of the Victorian past."[5] Thus, according to Johnston, Georgian poetry reveals "the loss of contact with contemporary reality."[6] In his protest against the revival — in the mid-1950s — of what he deems Georgian verse practices, Tambimuttu declares such poetry unconcerned with "the evocation of the experience and ideas òf the twentieth century."[7] And Anthony Thwaite, asserting as a familiar truth the preoccupation of Georgian poetry with "Olde Englande and Olde Englishnesse," expresses his dissatisfaction with that interest by observing that "The peculiar difficulties and complexities of modern life demanded new treatment in literature."[8]

As a consequence of their presumed indifference to the modern world, the Georgians have been readily contrasted with those poets who were aggressively Modernist, who claimed to have adjusted their themes and technique to the distinctive features of contemporary reality. Stephen Spender defines as Modernist those writers who deliberately set out "to invent a new literature as the result of their feeling that our age is in many respects unprecedented, and outside all the conventions of past literature and art."[9] But, according to received opinion, it was precisely this sense of history that the Georgians rejected. Noting this divided

---

4. H. M. [Harriet Monroe], "King George's Poets," *Poetry,* 16 (May 1920), 108-109.

5. John H. Johnston, *English Poetry of the First World War* (Princeton, 1964), p. 3.

6. *Ibid.*, p. 5. See also p. 28: "Most Georgian verse eschewed the real — the broad reality of contemporary life — and subsisted on rosy poetic mists."

7. Tambimuttu, "Poetry in A Gray Flannel Suit," *Poetry London-New York*, 1 (Winter 1956), 59.

8. Anthony Thwaite, *Contemporary English Poetry* (Philadelphia, 1961), p. 7.

9. Stephen Spender, *The Struggle of the Modern* (London, 1963), p. x.

view of the relationship between contemporary history and literature, Spender has named the Georgians "non-recognizers." "By
non-recognizers," he says, "I mean those who do not recognize the
modern situation. . . . The non-recognizer does not recognize the
world of today, or the need to deal with it." Spender calls the
Georgian poets "the classic examples in English in this century, of
non-recognizers."[10]

From Miss Monroe to Spender, the general disposition to view
the Georgians as nonrecognizers has made it easy enough for
critics to suppose that as the subject matter of the Georgians had
remained rural and preindustrial, so had their technique conserved
traditional prosodic forms and an archaic diction. Hence, one of
the newer dictionaries of literary terms says of Georgian poems
that their diction was, largely, "the traditional one of nineteenth-
century poetry, and their subject was nature in its more gentle
aspects."[11]   Critics, with the certainty of consensus, speak of the
Georgians as latter-day, if somewhat diminished, Romantics:

> It was during the reign of the Georgian Poets that Eliot published
> his first volumes of poetry, scandalizing those who got around to
> reading them. They astounded us. Here was no tweedy heartiness,
> no primrose echoes of Tennyson or Wordsworth, but an extreme
> sophistication, a truly urban poetry full of the ennui and melan-
> choly of great cities.[12]

And Moderns who reacted against the Georgians' apparent non-
recognition of the twentieth century had perforce to break
through and destroy — or at least deform — the traditional arti-
fices of the Georgian poet:

> What the idiomatic writing of Eliot and Pound did was to break
> through the crust of poeticisms which enclosed the Edwardians
> and Georgians. It enabled poets to write about modern ideas in a
> language open to the sights, sound, phrases, habits of thought
> which were contemporary.[13]

10. *Ibid.*, p. 159.
11. Karl Beckson and Arthur Ganz, *A Reader's Guide to Literary Terms* (New York,
1960), p. 68.
12. Leslie Paul, "The Elusive Genius of T. S. Eliot," *The Reporter*, 32 (April 22,
1965), 33.
13. Spender, *The Struggle of the Modern*, p. 195.

Thus, the pervasive charge that the Georgian poets were not in touch with the revolutionary character of the twentieth century is to be associated with the swelling debate — which commenced in the four or five years preceding the first World War in the manifestoes of the Futurists and the Imagists — over the altered nature of contemporary reality and the consequences of that transformation for the poet. Further, discussions of poetic technique, turning on the supposed opposition between convention and innovation, are properly related to this debate. And this polemic environment — with its strong suggestion of antinomous positions — has undoubtedly served to make the Georgians seem, by contrast, even more remote from modernity and even more docile in their adherence to the traditional forms and language of poetry.

Indeed, within this perspective, a more serious charge than non-recognition of the special qualities of their own century has been lodged against the Georgians: they have been indicted as escapist, as willfully regressive. In his description of the Georgian non-recognizer, Spender clearly strikes this note:

> He has the attitude to aesthetic enjoyment that the weekender has to the countryside. His true life, he maintains, is a world apart from the town, the office, the factory. What is "real" for him is not all this world of material involvement but the moment when the train slides past the last houses of the city of a Friday evening, and the green fields begin. The cottage, the hawthorn bush glimmering in the darkness — ghostly reflection of the Milky Way — such nature, he decides, is going to be, for him, reality. The means whereby he earns a livelihood, the benefits he consumes as a result of other people earning theirs, the lives of the industrial population — all these are "unreal," a nightmare imposed upon eternal values by frantic modern means.[14]

William York Tindall offers this judgment of the Georgians:

> They withdrew from reality, not to an ivory tower, but to an oast-house. Disheartened even in their happy time by its disorder and its noise, they sought peace among loud cattle and neglected gardens.[15]

14. *Ibid.*, p. 159.
15. William Y. Tindall, *Forces in Modern British Literature* (New York, 1947), pp. 372-373.

The same judgment is made, with unmistakable indignation, by Edith Batho and Bonamy Dobrée:

> They sang only of surface experiences, and their work was "scented with poetry." They withdrew themselves into worlds of birds and flowers, and crooned about them; or into worlds of their own sensations; or into worlds of meaningless antiquity. They were cut off from the major emotions of their age, and they did nothing towards clarifying the intellectual and emotional muddles of their time.[16]

The language of these descriptions suggests that the Georgians were somehow absurd, laughable. It plays a comic beam on them; and fixes them in an incongruous light as grown men behaving childishly or foolishly or helplessly, like Mr. Dick in *David Copperfield*. For example, Peter Quennell says of the Sitwells,

> they were apt to laugh at the rustic Georgian Poets, who seemed to pass their time sauntering and botanising around the muddy landscape that enclosed their country cottages, picking a celandine here, and there, over a five-barred gate, holding despondent conversations "with a lonely lamb."[17]

The interest of the Georgians in ballads and nursery rhymes has been regarded as a kind of grotesque infantilism.

The consequence of nonrecognition and escapism — if we may judge from the critical commentaries — has been the radically scaled-down quality of Georgian poetry. Like its ostensible subjects, it has been parochial, insubstantial, miniscular; hence, trivial, without significance, empty. In their supposed abdication of poetry's traditional claim to utter high truths, the Georgians appeared to reduce poetry to a polite avocation, pursued in an easy and unruffled way when a convenient opportunity presented itself. Spender, therefore, taxes them with reducing poetry to "a minor art like embroidery, to be done of a week-end in a country cottage."[18] It is this view that informs J. I. M. Stewart's criticism of the Georgians: "They lacked that radical passion for their

16. Edith C. Batho and Bonamy Dobrée, *The Victorians and After* (London, 1950), p. 72.

17. Peter Quennell, *The Sign of the Fish* (New York, 1960), p. 32.

18. Stephen Spender, *The Making of a Poem* (London, 1955), p. 14.

medium and its regular purification which marks the dedicated artist."[19] The same sense of what Georgianism entails persists in James Dickey's judgment on the work of Philip Booth: "Booth's is an American Georgian poetry, thinly descriptive, replete with easy answers, vacant, amiably bucolic."[20] The general implication here is that, while pleasant, Georgian poetry was without substance. Both admiration and criticism of the Georgians have, accordingly, often been referred to their technique, on the assumption that their work was essentially "decorative" in nature.[21]

It has been usual, as I have suggested, to associate Georgian technique with the verse practices of their Romantic and Victorian predecessors. David Wright states that the Georgians "based their technique on the sugary metres and diction of the nineteenth century."[22] And Joseph Warren Beach, speaking of a founder of Georgian poetry, notes that "Brooke is the surface of Keats, without Hyperion or the Grecian Urn."[23] Beach's qualification is significant. He concedes the Georgians' craftsmanship, their mastery of the style of the great Romantics and Victorians; but, having previously noted that "the strain of thinking" in Georgian poetry was "relaxed,"[24] he implies that the Georgians did not retain the striking intellectual and moral force of their distinguished predecessors. As Grierson and Smith put it, the Georgians "were content with small things; they did not emulate the lofty flights of the great Victorians."[25]

It is assumed by many critics of the Georgians that their predecessors, the great Romantic and Victorian poets, possessed a unified and comprehensive vision of the relation between man and the world, that it was this profound vision that underlay their

19. J. I. M. Stewart, *Eight Modern Writers* (Oxford, 1963), p. 14.

20. James Dickey, *The Suspect in Poetry* (Madison, Minn., 1964), p. 36.

21. See, for example, Christopher Hassall's *Biography of Edward Marsh* (New York, 1959): "By criticizing the emphasis given to expressiveness over the general conception and the substance of the thing said, [Squire] had detected the cause of that thinness of texture which later became a characteristic of much Georgian verse. It was decorative art" (p. 378).

22. David Wright, *Roy Campbell* (London, 1961), p. 11.

23. Joseph Warren Beach, "The Literature of the Nineteenth and the Early Twentieth Centuries, 1798 to the First World War," in *A History of English Literature*, ed. Hardin Craig (New York, 1950), p. 591.

24. *Ibid.*, p. 590.

25. Herbert J. C. Grierson and J. C. Smith, *A Critical History of English Poetry* (London, 1956), p. 495.

"simplest" lyrics and charged them with intensity and relevance. But, the argument continues, social change and the advance of scientific doctrine in the later nineteenth century shattered this vision. Thus, the empty formalism and the rural trivialities of Georgian poetry "reflect the decline of a once powerful imaginative vision" and the failure of the Georgians to replace it with a contemporary vision rising out of their contact with modern experience.[26] Scaled down, lacking both a world view and contact with its own time, Georgian poetry had evidently lost the intellectual and moral resonance of that older poetry to which it was apparently joined by its technique. Within the perspective of these assumptions about the relationship of Georgian poetry to its immediate past, it has been fashionable for critics to protest the disposition of the Georgians to restrict the scope of their observation; it has been usual to mark down the Georgians as deficient in the capacity to provide a wider reference for their experiences:

> Inability to suggest anything beyond the immediately comprehensible facts of existence was a fatal limitation in most of the Georgian poetry: it provided no enlargement of experience.[27]

Thus, by either nineteenth-century or Modernist literary standards, the Georgians appeared inadequate. They have been regarded — with nostalgia or pity or indignation — as a rear-guard action, as the last stragglers of a vanishing host, as the children of a bankrupt house who refuse to face the facts. Able to share neither the certitude of their fathers nor the despair of their contemporaries, they seem enervated:

> The effete pastoralism that was the characteristic element of Georgian poetry represented an attempt to escape from the realities of modern urban and industrial life.[28]

"Epigoni of the Victorian poetic achievement," the Georgians

---

26. See Johnston, *English Poetry of the First World War*, pp. 6-8.
27. A. C. Ward, *Twentieth-Century Literature* (London, 1956), pp. 189-190. See also John F. Lynen, *The Pastoral Art of Robert Frost* (New Haven, 1960), p. 177; and Samuel C. Chew, "The Nineteenth Century and After (1789-1939)," in *A Literary History of England*, ed. Albert C. Baugh (New York, 1948), p. 1579.
28. Johnston, *English Poetry of the First World War*, p. 28.

represented a "fatigued" tradition.[29] After likening the Georgians to the decadent aesthetes of the nineties, Louis MacNeice adds, "They were rightly determined to be less 'literary' than their predecessors but, dropping literature, they had not the strength to take up life."[30]   As C. Day Lewis puts it, the decline of English poetry in the later nineteenth century was followed early in the twentieth by "a period of very low vitality":

> The Georgian poets, a sadly pedestrian rabble, flocked along the road their fathers had built, pointing out to each other the beauty spots and ostentatiously drinking small-beer in a desperate effort to prove their virility.[31]

W. Y. Tindall pronounces Georgian poetry generally "sterile."[32]

Finally, in view of the great commercial success of the five volumes of *Georgian Poetry*, Georgianism has connoted a kind of formula for broad approval by the popular audience for poetry. In its use of conventionalized poetic diction and forms, in the supposedly gentle and uncontroversial character of its themes, in its presumed mediocrity, Georgian poetry gratified perfectly — we are told — the mindless and sentimental audience for poetry. The Georgians were regularly denounced by the Modernists as panderers to the public's taste for "easy" and reassuring poetry. One of the more influential editors of Modernist poetry describes Georgian poetry as "easily 'communicable' since everything is made immediately apparent."[33]   Although no Modernist, Roy Campbell makes this savage comment — in his poem "Georgian Spring" — on the commercial success of the Georgians:

> The publishers put on their best apparel
> To sell the public everything it wants —
> A thousand meek soprano voices carol
> The loves of homosexuals or plants.[34]

In the light of this unfortunate reputation for vapid traditionalism, it is scarcely surprising that critics who have perceived

---

29. Wright, *Roy Campbell*, p. 10.
30. Louis Macneice, *Modern Poetry* (Oxford, 1938), p. 9.
31. C. Day Lewis, *A Hope for Poetry* (Oxford, 1944), p. 2.
32. Tindall, *Forces in Modern British Literature*, p. 373.
33. Tambimuttu, "Poetry in A Gray Flannel Suit," p. 59.
34. Roy Campbell, *The Collected Poems of Roy Campbell* (London, 1949), I, 181.

merit in the writings of, say, Davies or de la Mare or Blunden or Graves have usually sought to exculpate them from membership in the Georgian movement. C. K. Stead has taken proper note of this strategy:

> It is common, since the Georgians are out of favour, for critics to insist of any Georgian poet they admire that he did not really belong to the movement. Professor Pinto writes that Robert Graves "really had no connection with the Georgian fold"; David Daiches insists that the trench poets who appeared in later issues of the Anthology did not belong there; and a chorus of critics begins its remarks on D. H. Lawrence's poetry by saying that he was "not a Georgian." [35]

> Some critics have argued that Edward Thomas was not a Georgian. . . . This I think is only because any critic writing of Thomas at some length wants the poems treated with respect, and knows that for years "Georgian" has been a term of abuse. [36]

One form of this strategy is the denial that Georgian poetry constituted a "movement," the insistence that the Georgians can be most accurately characterized in terms of their diversity. For example, committed as he is to the Modernist position yet determined to record his sense of de la Mare's merits, Spender takes this line:

> When a great many misconceptions have been cleared away, it may be seen that the Georgian poets should be judged by their achievements [i.e., as individuals], not as a movement related to the 1920's or the 1930's. [37]

Another form of the strategy protests the vagueness and ambiguity of the name "Georgian." Thus Richard J. Stonesifer, eager — in his critical biography of W. H. Davies — to discriminate between the "natural simplicity" of Davies and the "artificial simplicity" of his fellow Georgians, questions the suitability of the name:

> From the beginning the term "Georgian" was a misnomer. First, it is confusing, for most of the earliest contributors may more properly be called Edwardians. Also the term is vague (even

35. Stead, *The New Poetic*, pp. 87-88.
36. *Ibid.*, p. 101. See also John F. Danby, "Edward Thomas," *Critical Quarterly*, 1 (Winter 1959), 308.
37. Spender, *The Making of a Poem*, p. 150.

Marsh called it his "proud ambiguous adjective"), and since the participating poets neither had nor sought to have a common denominator, the use of the label created confusion.[38]

Robert Graves is a particularly clear instance of a poet dissociated from Georgianism by his admiring critics. Either, we are told, his relationship to the Georgians was adventitious, without genuine significance; or he was, indeed, early dedicated to them but, seeing the error of his Georgian ways, turned to worthier views of the nature and function of poetry. Douglas Day subscribes to the latter alternative in his disposition to regard Graves, chronologically, as first a Georgian and later a good poet. In his account of the Georgian stage in Graves's career, Day states the "official" view of the Georgians: they practiced a "tepid and uninspired brand of poetry"; they are vestiges of the "worn-out tradition" of Romanticism.[39] And surely, Day suggests, whatever one's estimate of the poet who now serves the White Goddess, his poems could hardly be described as tepid, uninspired, faded.

As the influence of Modernist poetry — and, more specifically, of Pound and Eliot — began to diminish in the 1950s, however, a kind of Georgian revival commenced. Spender was among the first to remark this renewed interest: "Forty years after the appearance of the first volume in 1912 . . . there are signs of a revival of interest in *Georgian Poetry*."[40] In 1961, a close observer of the English literary scene provided this comment on "a very promising poet":

> As his recent reviews show, he admires (of all people!) the Georgian poets. And he is not alone among the young in this, as is shown by the fact that only the other day the B.B.C. Third Programme devoted a whole program to the Georgians. For thirty years "Georgian" has been a term of abuse: it looks now as though it may not be one much longer.[41]

And, more recently, Horace Gregory has both noted this Georgian revival and suggested, provocatively, that it may be associated with the new estimation of Graves's importance:

38. Richard J. Stonesifer, *W. H. Davies: A Critical Biography* (London, 1963), p. 98.
39. Douglas Day, *Swifter Than Reason* (Chapel Hill, 1963), pp. 18-19.
40. Spender, *The Making of a Poem*, p. 145.
41. Walter Allen, "A Literary Letter From London," *New York Times Book Review*, September 17, 1961, p. 40.

Georgian poetry, which fell out of fashion in the 1930's, is now undergoing not only a critical reassessment – partly because of the ascendency of Robert Graves – but also something of a revival. [42]

Now that the Georgians are less frequently dismissed as hopelessly retrograde, it has become possible to entertain less tendentious and fuller discussions of them. Several recent studies, accordingly, have served to call into question and to correct the almost vulgar caricatures of the Georgians that have heretofore passed for literary history and criticism. The conventional characterization of the Georgian movement has been sharply corrected in two independently conceived studies, C. K. Stead's *The New Poetic* (1964) and Robert H. Ross's *The Georgian Revolt* (1965). And the conventional view of the Georgian poets has been rendered far less simple and stereotyped by Christopher Hassall's biographies of Edward Marsh (1959) and Rupert Brooke (1964), Richard Stonesifer's biography of W. H. Davies and Patrick Howarth's of Sir John Squire (1963), Joy Grant's study of Harold Monro (1967), Timothy Rogers's vignette of Brooke (1971), and John Sherwood's biography of Flecker (1973); by the Abbott-Bertram edition of Gordon Bottomley's correspondence with Paul Nash (1955), the R. G. Thomas edition of Edward Thomas's letters to Bottomley (1968), and the Geoffrey Keynes edition of Brooke's letters (1968). Coming, significantly, one upon the other after a long silence on the Georgians, these books collectively compel a revised perception of the Georgian program and achievement. Stead, indeed, concludes his discussion on a note of defiance:

> If the evidence here assembled is accepted, it is no longer possible, for example, to "write off" the Georgians with that confidence which has become almost mechanical in recent criticism. [43]

As the title of Ross's study indicates, the Georgian movement was rebellious rather than conformist. It was a revolt against Romantic and Victorian conceptions of poetry and the contemporary representatives of those conceptions: against "public"

---

42. Horace Gregory, " 'The Best of All Is to Live Poetry,' " *New York Times Book Review*, August 30, 1964, p. 4.
43. Stead, *The New Poetic*, pp. 188-189.

poetry, on the one hand, and "pure" poetry, on the other; against the moralist and the aesthete. Relatedly, it was a revolt against poetic mannerism, against the continuing fashionability — in the first decade of the twentieth century — of archaic and heavily "poetic" language. It rebelled against poetry written by rhetoricians, sentimentalists, and sensualists. Thus, the Georgians were hardly the docile and fatigued legatees of nineteenth-century poetic tradition. That distinction fell rather to poets like William Watson, Stephen Phillips, and Alfred Austin, whom the Georgians thought fully representative of the low state into which English poetry had fallen in the first decade of the new century.

This perception of the Georgians' stance has been obscured by immoderately generalized — as well as by pejorative — use of the term "Georgian." It has been used in an almost purely chronological sense to refer to any writing produced during the reign of George V (1910-1936), that is, the sense in which literary historians refer to the Georgian periods of the eighteenth and nineteenth centuries. The term has also been used, more specifically, to describe virtually all those writers who sought to bring a fresh spirit into early twentieth-century British literature, that is, the sense in which Bloomsbury was a part of the Georgian literary scene. Ross uses the term in this sense to describe, with what he regards as equal appropriateness, the work of Pound and Rupert Brooke, of Richard Aldington and Lascelles Abercrombie.[44] Further, since the term was given currency by the success of Edward Marsh's *Georgian Poetry* anthologies, it has been applied — with yet greater strictness — to Marsh's group alone and thus held to be inapplicable to the members of the Imagist group. In this sense, therefore, the term has been applied to Brooke and Abercrombie but not to Pound and Aldington. And, as the ultimate semantic refinement, the term has been judged specifically applicable by both Stead and Ross to only the early members of the Marsh group, the poets who dominated the first three volumes of *Georgian Poetry*, as distinct from the Neo-Georgian group associated with Sir John Squire whose influence decidedly altered the nature of the last two volumes.[45]

44. Ross, *The Georgian Revolt*, p. 22.
45. Ross has elected to use the term in all of these four senses, but happily is sufficiently precise in his usage to avoid the customary confusions. He uses the term very broadly, i.e., in the first two senses, in his first chapter, a survey of the literary scene in

The term "Georgian" is most accurately and usefully employed in these last two, more specific, senses. That is, since the poets gathered about Edward Marsh are properly to be differentiated from both traditionalist and Modernist poets of the same period, I call them alone by the name that Marsh was the first to use and that he used restrictively. And, since there were two distinct stages of Georgian poetry, I distinguish between the first stage or generation in which Marsh was himself the central figure and the second in which — albeit with Marsh's approval — Squire was the shaping force. By the "Georgian poetic," then, I mean the literary principles of the early Marsh group, the first stage of Georgian poetry.

1911: "The term 'Georgian,' as it is used in this context and as I shall use it henceforth to the end of this chapter, has no implications of a poetic coterie or school. It is used in its widest and most literal sense, i.e., as a historical tag to describe that poetry written after the accession of George V. Cf. 'Edwardian.' In this use of the term, obviously Ezra Pound and Richard Aldington are to be considered as much 'Georgian' poets as Rupert Brooke or W. H. Davies. As will be made clear below (ch. 6), the term is susceptible of a more restricted definition, namely to describe those poets who were contributors to any of the five volumes of Edward Marsh's anthology" (The Georgian Revolt, p. 244, n. 20). Turning from his introductory survey of the new poetry to the Marsh group, he provides this caveat: "Obviously, the term 'Georgian,' as it is used here [chap. 6] and will be used in subsequent chapters, has a more restricted meaning than heretofore (cf. ch. 1). I am beginning to use the adjective not in its merely generic or temporal sense, but to describe specifically the work of those poets chosen for representation in G.P. I and II"(The Georgian Revolt, p. 259, n. 5). Subsequently, Ross introduces the terminological distinction between Georgian and Neo-Georgian poetry (pp. 162 ff.). As Ross acknowledges (p. 266, n. 58), his distinction between the two Georgian schools was anticipated by Herbert Palmer in Post-Victorian Poetry (London, 1938).

2

THE INTELLECTUAL BACKGROUND OF GEORGIAN POETRY

Georgian poetry issued from the friendship of Edward Marsh with Rupert Brooke and from their collateral friendships. It was Brooke who conceived the idea of offering the public a volume of the new poetry; and it was Marsh who defined the principles of inclusion, gave the volume its name, and ensured its publication. Above all, it was Marsh who asserted virtually absolute editorial control over the five successive volumes called *Georgian Poetry*, although the character of the last volumes was scarcely consistent with that of the early ones.[1]

The first stage of Georgian poetry is most clearly identified with the first two volumes of *Georgian Poetry* (published in 1912 and 1915). As Ross points out, "From the historical point of view *Georgian Poetry* I and II are both of a piece; their differences are largely differences in degree, their similarities inherent and fundamental."[2] He adds, indeed, "Taken together, then, *Georgian Poetry* I and II afford some evidence for claiming the existence of a specifically 'Georgian' poetic."[3] The poets most central to this first stage were Brooke, Lascelles Abercrombie, Gordon Bottomley, William H. Davies, Walter de la Mare, and Wilfrid Gibson. And other important contributors, like James Elroy

---

1. The first account of the circumstances attending the birth of *Georgian Poetry* appears in Marsh's "Memoir" of Brooke, written in August 1915 but — owing to the objections of Brooke's mother — not published until July 1918. See Edward Marsh, ed., *Rupert Brooke: The Collected Poems* (London, 1918), pp. lxxv-lxxvi. See also Edward Marsh, *A Number of People* (New York, 1939), pp. 320-321, where Marsh simply quotes from the account in his "Memoir" of Brooke; Christopher Hassall, *A Biography of Edward Marsh* (New York, 1959), pp. 189-204; Christopher Hassall, *Rupert Brooke* (London, 1964), pp. 359-360. The most detailed account of the launching of *Georgian Poetry* is to be found in Robert H. Ross's *The Georgian Revolt, 1910-1922* (Carbondale, Ill., 1965), pp. 97-114.
2. Ross, *The Georgian Revolt*, p. 115.
3. *Ibid.*, p. 117.

Flecker and D. H. Lawrence, were by no means as anomalous as historians of Georgian poetry have usually indicated. Yet these poets and their editor produced no manifesto, stated no explicit program. Thus, the special character of their affiliation must be sought elsewhere; and it is with the peculiarly deceptive figure of Edward Marsh that we must begin.

Understanding Marsh is crucial to a proper understanding of Georgian poetry because he has been more closely identified with it than has anyone else and because he impressed upon it so pervasively, albeit implicitly, the cast of his intellectual and temperamental loyalties. Unfortunately, Marsh's actual loyalties have been seldom recognized, so that his "own view" of Georgian poetry "from his editorial chair . . . has been too often misunderstood."[4] Indeed, the misunderstanding of Marsh may be proposed as one of the important sources of the widespread misunderstanding of Georgian poetry. Marsh has long been stereotypically regarded as a rather pompous, mindless conservative and as a prim aesthete, a monocled dandy who failed pathetically to mark the vital artistic, philosophical, and social currents of his own time. This view of Marsh has helped to form the generally unflattering response to Georgian poetry; and Georgian poetry has, in turn, stood in apparent corroboration of this view of Marsh. Thus, Peter Quennell says of Marsh that "his tastes in literature were conservative and he did not pretend to enjoy a poem unless he was sure that he had understood its meaning."[5] And W. Y. Tindall offers this equation of Marsh's alleged conventionalism with the character of Georgian poetry:

> Georgian poetry . . . is that part of contemporary poetry which appealed to the taste of Edward Marsh. As might be supposed, this taste was conservative. Interesting poets, thought radical, were carefully excluded as those were who, face to face with reality, found rhythms for it and suitable metaphors. Intended to mean up-to-date, "Georgian" came to mean reactionary.[6]

To be sure, Marsh has himself called attention to the force of tradition in his rearing, to the maternally enforced orthodoxy that

4. Hassall, *A Biography of Edward Marsh*, p. x.
5. Peter Quennell, *The Sign of the Fish* (New York, 1960), p. 145.
6. William Y. Tindall, *Forces in Modern British Literature* (New York, 1947), p. 373. See also Frank Swinnerton, *Figures in the Foreground* (London, 1963), p. 22.

so carefully and insistently directed his early education along narrowly Victorian lines. Born in 1872, he said that — owing to his mother — his "home-education . . . was at least thirty years out of date."[7] He likened his home atmosphere to that described by Edmund Gosse in *Father and Son,* although Gosse was twenty-four years his senior. As a boy, he read Shakespeare in Dr. Bowdler's edition, was quite overwhelmed by *Marmion* and *The Lay of the Last Minstrel,* and was moved to tears by the beauty of *Paradise Lost* as it was read to him by his mother.[8] But it was his attachment to Cambridge University that proved genuinely transforming. It was at Cambridge that the strenuous effort of the "angelic" Jane Marsh to inculcate a firmly Victorian rectitude in her "Eddie" was thoroughly undone. It was at Cambridge that Marsh's characteristic habits of mind were definitively set.

Surveying the temper of English life at the end of the nineties — the decade in which Marsh commenced his close relationship with Cambridge — Frank Swinnerton suggests a pervasive sense of the weakening and deterioration of the Victorian establishment. He refers to military and political humiliations abroad, to an increasing lack of confidence in the superiority and unremitting progress of the British Empire at home. "We were," he says, "certainly uneasy and full of self-criticism."[9] Indeed, Swinnerton associates Kipling's eclipse at this time with a swelling antipathy toward imperialist complacency which extended to its architects and apologists. Swinnerton describes the "new trend" in English thought at the beginning of the twentieth century as growing "out of a perception that, even if one disliked them, one could not and should not ignore facts."[10] And the Cambridge at which Marsh arrived in 1891 was the intellectual center of this new critical spirit, this new mood of intense inquiry. The misgivings Jane Marsh experienced in consequence of her son's emancipation from her immediate supervision proved well founded. On Marsh's first Sunday home, after his taking up residence at Trinity, he "talked

7. Marsh, *A Number of People,* p. 14.

8. *Ibid.,* pp. 16-17.

9. Frank Swinnerton, *Background with Chorus* (London, 1956), p. 16.

10. *Ibid.,* p. 26. In a Cambridge undergraduate magazine of the 1890s, one might predictably find a parody of Kipling's rugged imperial style. See *The Cambridge A.B.C.,* 3 (June 11, 1894), 47-50. Marsh's set of this journal may be seen in the Berg Collection of the New York Public Library.

enthusiastically" of his new friends, among whom he already numbered Bertrand Russell.[11]

At home Russell had perforce concealed his utilitarianism and agnosticism. He declares that, when he once acknowledged himself a utilitarian, he "was met with such a blast of ridicule" that he never again confided his opinions at home. He found, however, that Cambridge opened to him "a new world of infinite delight." Of his going up to Cambridge in 1890 Russell observes, "For the first time I found that, when I uttered my thoughts, they seemed to be accepted as worth considering."[12] Similarly, although the philosopher G. E. Moore had become an agnostic before his enrollment at Trinity College in 1892, he says, "Until I went to Cambridge, I had had no idea how exciting life could be."[13] Marsh, warmly befriending both and other Cantabrigians equally zealous to pursue truth wherever it led and whomever it affronted, described his circle at Cambridge thus:

> We were all tingling with intellectual curiosity, arguing on every subject in the firm belief that we should thus arrive at Truth; mostly hard workers, for the sake of the work, with little thought of our 'careers'; keen politicians, nearly all Liberals.[14]

Such a circle might be depended upon to welcome the new spirit of realism and uncompromising honesty in any of its manifestations. Consequently, it is hardly surprising that in 1892 Marsh enthusiastically reviewed, for the *Cambridge Observer*, the first performance in England of Ibsen's *A Doll's House*. In 1893 he reviewed, again with evident enthusiasm, the English production of *Ghosts*. And the young reviewer learned that the translator of

11. Hassall, *A Biography of Edward Marsh*, p. 26.
12. Bertrand Russell, "My Mental Development," in *The Philosophy of Bertrand Russell*, ed. Paul A. Schilpp (New York, 1951), p. 8. He further characterized the Cambridge of the 1890s as a place "where independence of mind could exist undeterred." Bertrand Russell, *Portraits from Memory and Other Essays* (New York, 1965), p. 66.
13. G. E. Moore, "An Autobiography," in *The Philosophy of G. E. Moore*, ed. Paul A. Schilpp (Evanston and Chicago, 1942), p. 13.
14. Marsh, *A Number of People*, p. 45. See also Hassall, *A Biography of Edward Marsh*, pp. 66-67. For excellent accounts of Cambridge rationalism, see Noel Annan, *Leslie Stephen* (Cambridge, Mass., 1952), pp. 130-149; and C. D. Broad, "The Local Historical Background of Contemporary Cambridge Philosophy," in *British Philosophy in the Mid-Century: A Cambridge Symposium*, ed. C. A. Mace (London, 1966), pp. 13-61.

these Ibsen plays, William Archer, had read his reviews and "was confident they had done much to further the cause."[15] Marsh's literary taste was, at least then, scarcely governed by prudence, decorousness, and an unthinking acquiescence in tradition. Rather, he seems to have been drawn to literature that was independently conceived and to artists whose dedication to truth and to their art led them to disregard public expectations. These predilections were brought into relief through Marsh's close association with the early thought of Russell and Moore. Christopher Hassall observed that "the climate of thought which centered in Moore and Russell in the middle 'nineties found no more characteristic product than Eddie Marsh."[16]

During their overlapping undergraduate careers at Cambridge, both Russell and Moore were not only close friends of Marsh but thought him worthy of intellectual cultivation. In an intimate letter of 1894 to Alys Pearsall Smith, Russell speaks of having returned to Cambridge to deliver a philosophical paper at a meeting of the Apostles Society. He writes, "I have left my paper behind as Marsh and Sanger want to read it over again." "I always speak the truth to Marsh," he adds, noting that he "stayed up till 2 talking to Marsh."[17] In reminiscences of his undergraduate days at Cambridge, Russell describes Marsh as his "close friend."[18] And the five letters extant from Moore to Marsh — characteristically emphasizing complete honesty in outlook and clarity in the expression of one's views — assert a relationship both comradely and didactic.[19] If their relationships with Marsh grew more remote in the early decades of the twentieth century, it was very likely because — at the time their interests were shifting preeminently into technical philosophy — Marsh had commenced his long career in government service. This vocational choice, which was soon to link Marsh with Winston Churchill, must surely have strained Marsh's relationship with Russell, especially during the first World

15. Hassall, *A Biography of Edward Marsh*, pp. 29-30, 36, 42.
16. *Ibid.*, p. 66.
17. Bertrand Russell, *The Autobiography of Bertrand Russell: 1872-1914* (London, 1967), p. 107. Russell observes that he "was at this time very intimate with Eddie Marsh" (p. 108).
18. Russell, *Portraits from Memory*, p. 73.
19. Letters from G. E. Moore to Marsh, dated March 17, 1896; April 12, 1896; April 17, 1896; September 29, 1896; and October 18, 1897, in the Berg Collection of the New York Public Library.

War. Russell's criticism in 1916 of the British government's method of punishing conscientious objectors to military conscription led to his being prosecuted and fined by the government and removed by the Trinity College Council from his lectureship at Cambridge. He was prosecuted a second time in 1918 for making a statement prejudicial to the government's relations with the United States, and this time sentenced to six months' imprisonment. Nevertheless, according to Hassall, Marsh's philosophical views coincided with Russell's, save on the issue of pacifism. Indeed, on occasion Russell undertook at Marsh's request to answer philosophic inquiries directed at Marsh.[20]

Although both Russell and Moore were under Hegelian influence during their undergraduate years at Cambridge, they were neither conventional nor uncritical idealists. British idealism, at the end of the past century, was of course antimaterialist; but it was not engaged in a pious effort to revive the Platonic tradition. Rather, British idealists like T. H. Green, F. H. Bradley, and J. E. McTaggart were then occupied in pointing out that the materialist position, which in popularized utilitarian form seemed to undergird the self-serving behavior of Victorian entrepreneurs and imperialists, rested on no firm metaphysical and epistemological foundations. Lord Lindsay has remarked of Green and his fellow idealists that "They were growing up when the reigning philosophy in the universities was that of John Stuart Mill." They perceived that this philosophy "was really an eclecticism which had inspiring elements in it, but was incapable of producing fruitful social or political principles"; and they concluded that "Utilitarianism or Associationism or Empiricism had to be fought all along the line."[21] And T. S. Eliot has rightly observed that Bradley's *Ethical Studies* was "not merely a demolition of the Utilitarian theory of conduct but an attack upon the whole Utilitarian mind":

> For Utilitarianism was, as every reader of Arnold knows, a great temple in Philistia. And of this temple Arnold hacked at the ornaments and cast down the images. . . . But Bradley, in his

20. Hassall, *A Biography of Edward Marsh*, p. 509.
21. A. D. Lindsay, "T. H. Green and the Idealists," in *The Social and Political Ideas of Some Representative Thinkers of the Victorian Age*, ed. F. J. C. Hearnshaw (London, 1933), p. 153.

philosophical critique of Utilitarianism, undermined the foundations.[22]

Utilitarian ethical directives could be shown, on close inspection, to rest on no adequate definitions of knowledge and experience. This discovery seemed to the teachers of Russell and Moore manifest evidence of the impercipience and even the meaninglessness of the utilitarian and other empiricist formulations of truth. Thus, the mood of these idealists was skeptical, their method increasingly objective and analytic. They were disposed to be wary of universal propositions, of anything that purported to be a philosophical system.[23] They taught so well and their students were so amenable to this new "tough-minded" style of philosophy that, by the beginning of the new century, Moore and Russell had overthrown even the critical idealism of their mentors. Asserting their independence, Moore and Russell were prepared to restrict radically the scope of philosophic discussion to arrive at what might more confidently and defensibly be described as truth. From their teachers and the generally liberating climate of thought at Cambridge, Moore and Russell derived the passion for clarity and the abhorrence of windy abstractions which they helped importantly to make such distinctive features of Marsh's intellectual orientation.

The Moore and Russell by whom Marsh was so deeply affected had abandoned the search for grandiose syntheses of thought in favor of minute, painstaking analyses of carefully limited segments of experience and perception. They were passionately preoccupied with knowing and stating truths in essentially common-sense terms. They regarded truth as plural, and hence they were skeptical of any sort of philosophical or religious monism. Thus, they were committed to a correspondence — not to a coherence — theory of truth. Following William James's famous distinction, Russell did not hesitate to declare himself a "tough-minded"

22. T. S. Eliot, *For Lancelot Andrewes* (London, 1970), pp. 58-59. First published in 1928.

23. In the "Preface" to his *Principles of Logic* (Oxford, 1883), Bradley said that "We want no system-making or systems home-grown or imported." Indeed, as Eliot has noted, in each of his three books Bradley explicitly disclaimed the construction of a system as his intention (*For Lancelot Andrewes*, pp. 53-54). In this connection, Herbert Spencer's *System of Synthetic Philosophy* and Ernst Haeckel's *The Riddle of the Universe* were obvious targets of idealist criticism.

philosopher.[24]   And in a letter to the poet Robert Nichols, written
at Marsh's request, Russell declared knowledge "all vague and
approximate; the more vague, the less likely to be mistaken":

> Yes, I regard metaphysics as dead. It is true that without meta-
> physics there can be no certainty; but as there is no certain
> metaphysics, that doesn't help much. As to whether we "know"
> anything, it is necessary to define "knowing," which is a difficult
> matter.[25]

The monist, however, regarded truth as systemic, as the aggre-
gate property of all the propositions that comprised his system, so
that all of his propositions were necessarily related to each other.
He sought "to deduce the rich diversity of experience from some
single principle, whether it was mechanical action, as in the case of
the materialists, or the necessities of thought, as in the case of the
Hegelians."[26] This claim accounted for the certitude and even the
sublimity of much monistic thought; but it also accounted for its
abstraction and its failures to reflect accurately the texture of
reality, deficiencies that arose from the monist's reluctance to
describe any single proposition as of itself true or false. In stressing
their skeptical pluralism Moore, Russell, and their circle were
questioning the monistic certitude upon which Victorian rectitude
and complacency rested. Whether in its materialist or its idealist
forms, monism was to be questioned and a more honest transcript
of reality provided. It was this philosophical debate that significantly informed the sense of liberation then extant at Cambridge.
Thus, while holidaying at a German pension in the summer of
1894, Marsh could write to Moore that the detachment from his
"ordinary way of life" afforded him a new view of himself:

> The thing that surprised me was the way in which I turned out
> not to have any moral prejudices at all about the way in which
> other people ought to behave, and very few about how I ought to
> behave myself.[27]

24. See Bertrand Russell, *Philosophical Essays* (London, 1966), p. 113. The book
was first published in 1910.
25. Letter from Bertrand Russell to Robert Nichols, dated June 17, 1923, in the
Berg Collection of the New York Public Library. Cf. Hassall, *A Biography of Edward
Marsh*, p. 509.
26. John Passmore, *A Hundred Years of Philosophy* (London, 1966), p. 47.
27. Hassall, *A Biography of Edward Marsh*, p. 54.

Moore and Russell wished to confront experience directly, to know its truths with as little distortion as possible; and they were consequently less disposed to wield Occam's razor than to find the "real" questions and to think them through independently. Moore's philosophy, in particular, is directed toward the achievement of an unmediated perception of reality: an effort that rested on a common-sense faith in the existence of the external world, a capacity to think out one's sense of his experience in that world, and a strong disposition to disregard the received truths of conventional wisdom. John Maynard Keynes has provided an authoritative description of the intellectual orientation developed at Cambridge under the profound influence of Moore in the years immediately following the close undergraduate association of Marsh with Moore:

> Nothing mattered except states of mind, our own and other people's of course, but chiefly our own. These states of mind were not associated with action or achievement or with consequences. They consisted in timeless, passionate states of contemplation and communion, largely unattached to "before" and "after." . . . How did we know what states of mind were good? This was a matter of direct inspection, of direct unanalysable intuition about which it was useless and impossible to argue.[28]

Speaking of *Principia Ethica* (1903), Keynes said, "It conveys the beauty of the literalness of Moore's mind, the pure and passionate intensity of his vision, *un*fanciful and *un*dressed-up."[29] For Moore, most notably, fineness of perception demanded in turn a method of analysis and a style of discourse that would accurately represent — without blurring or distortion — what sensibility had reported.[30] It is significant that, in referring to J. E. McTaggart as the philosopher who most influenced him during his undergradu-

28. J. M. Keynes, *Two Memoirs* (London, 1949), pp. 83-84.

29. *Ibid.*, p. 94. Keynes's portrayal of Moore's influence has been usefully qualified. See Leonard Woolf, *Sowing: An Autobiography of the Years 1880 to 1904* (New York, 1960). Woolf denies Keynes's contention that Moore's disciples were indifferent to matters of action and conduct.

30. For a summary of Moore's philosophic values and method, see Albert W. Levi, *Philosophy and the Modern World* (Bloomington, Ind., 1959), pp. 448-462. See also the chapter on Moore and Russell in John Passmore, *A Hundred Years of Philosophy*, pp. 203-241; and A. J. Ayer, *Russell and Moore: The Analytical Heritage* (London, 1971).

ate studies, Moore calls particular attention to McTaggart's "constant insistence on clearness — on trying to give a precise meaning to philosophical expressions."[31] Keynes offered this characterization of Moore's method of analysis:

> you could hope to make essentially vague notions clear by using precise language about them and asking exact questions. It was a method of discovery by the instrument of impeccable grammar and an unambiguous dictionary.[32]

It must be stressed that Moore and Russell were not merely common-sense realists who restricted their concept of experience to verifiable knowledge. Their greater loyalty was to the actual texture of experience, which might indeed be said to possess certain general qualities at first only intuitively apprehended. The job of the philosopher for them was to prevent the opposed monistic tendencies toward abstraction from experience, on the one hand, and rigid empiricism, on the other, from obscuring a clear view of the true character of reality. Hence, we have Russell's statement that reality consists of concrete particulars and Platonic universals.[33] Accordingly, Russell's absorbing interest in mathematics and logic, early in his career, did not preclude his sympathetic understanding of mysticism. Russell has made this comment on the range of his thought and method:

> My method invariably is to start from something vague but puzzling, something which seems indubitable but which I cannot express with any precision. I go through a process which is like that of first seeing something with the naked eye and then examining it through a microscope. I find that by fixity of attention divisions and distinctions appear where none at first was visible, just as through a microscope you can see the bacilli in impure water which without the microscope are not discernible. . . . This applies not only to the structure of physical things, but quite as much to concepts. "Knowledge," for example, as commonly used is a very imprecise term covering a number of

31. Schilpp, *The Philosophy of G. E. Moore*, p. 18.
32. Keynes, *Two Memoirs*, p. 88. Passmore says of Moore that "no writer has ever sought so desperately to achieve utter clarity and utter simplicity, unless it be Gertrude Stein" (*A Hundred Years of Philosophy*, p. 204).
33. Schilpp, *The Philosophy of Bertrand Russell*, p. 12. Cf. Morton White, *The Age of Analysis* (Boston, 1955), pp. 23-24.

different things and a number of stages from certainty to slight
probability. It seems to me that philosophical investigation, as far
as I have experience of it, starts from that curious and unsatisfactory state of mind in which one feels complete certainty
without being able to say what one is certain of.[34]

Similarly, Moore combined a skeptical rationalism with an open-
ness to imaginative or spiritual intuitions. The skeptical side of
Moore was constantly questioning conventional philosophic tenets
and returning them to the myriad details and complex alternatives
of ordinary experience. But the other side of Moore unfailingly
recognized that there is far more richness in human perception
than can be satisfactorily explained in rational terms. This side of
Moore trusted, indeed depended upon, intuition and imaginative
insight. Thus, if one were concerned to place these two philoso-
phers — who acted so directly upon Marsh — in relation to their
contemporaries and predecessors, they might properly be
described as "centrist" in their rejection of extreme and single
positions to gain a broader, less obstructed angle of vision, as in
Principia Ethica where Moore demonstrates that *both* materialistic
and metaphysical ethics commit the "naturalistic fallacy."

Their philosophical position, moreover, had its religious, political, and literary correlatives at Cambridge. It provided the ration-
ale for a reflective, intellectually substantial agnosticism, into
which Marsh was promptly drawn. Hassall relates that Cambridge
seemed, to Marsh's evangelical mother, to be turning him away
from religion altogether, for the friends who most influenced him
there were agnostic.[35] It also seemed to find a centrist political
equivalent in the Liberal Party, with its appeal to specific issues as
opposed to the complacently generalized toryism of the Unionists;
and it stimulated receptivity to the Fabians' analytical critique of
the "immutable laws" of classical economic theory. Finally, it
served to endow art with intrinsic value. As distinct from the views
that the value of art is pragmatically determined by its moral
utility or that art is unconcerned with reality and lacks utility,
Russell posited the differentiation of art from ethics and science:

As to the functions of the artist and the scientist: the scientist is

34. Bertrand Russell, *My Philosophical Development* (New York, 1959), p. 133.
35. Hassall, *A Biography of Edward Marsh*, p. 46.

concerned only with knowledge, which is valuable chiefly as a means. As an end, it has some value, but only as one among ends. As ends, the artist's ends seem to me better. Blake, of course, is a moralist as well as an artist, which complicates matters. It is clear that to commend an ethic successfully, artistic gifts are required; but that is outside the value of art as such.

In the "best instances" of literature, Russell found "a quality of magic or enchantment, which seems to flood the world with golden sunlight." Such literature provided a strange sort of "delight in life and the world," a delight growing out of the capacity of art to irradiate the shadowy ambiguities of experience. And for Russell this delight was something "good in itself": neither hedonistic nor the means to some moral end, but an oblique kind of knowing that richly complemented the discursive reason.[36]

With Moore, he regarded art as a peculiarly effective means of embodying those perceptual states most fully available to the intuition and the imagination. Although Moore seems to blur the relation of ethics to art in *Principia Ethica* by including the enjoyment of beautiful objects among the states of consciousness properly describable as good, he carefully distinguishes them in his concluding chapter.[37] They believed that the value of art, as of philosophy, resided in the independence of the observer and in the accuracy and the intensity of his statement. Art ought not, therefore, to ideologize, on the one hand, or to become "pure" by withdrawing from experience, on the other. True art, rather, is what expands and clarifies those events in human consciousness which could not have been as adequately expressed in nonartistic form.

The philosophical position of Moore and Russell early in their careers, with its correlative postures, has been long known to have been the principal intellectual influence upon the Bloomsbury group. J. K. Johnstone, for example, has demonstrated the extent to which the philosophy of Moore in particular served to shape the Bloomsbury aesthetic.[38] Yet the equally pervasive intellectual

36. Letter from Bertrand Russell to Robert Nichols, dated June 17, 1923, in the Berg Collection of the New York Public Library.
37. G. E. Moore, *Principia Ethica* (Cambridge, 1903), pp. 201-202.
38. J. K. Johnstone, *The Bloomsbury Group* (New York, 1954). See especially chapter 2, "Bloomsbury Philosophy."

influence they exercised upon Marsh and his "centrist" Georgians has remained virtually unnoticed; and, as a consequence, understanding of the Georgian poetic has been imperfect.

Like the chief members of the Bloomsbury group, the founders of Georgian poetry were Cambridge men whose religious views were agnostic, whose political views were liberal, whose literary views were both anti-Victorian and anti-Decadent, and whose basic intellectual orientation derived from Moore and Russell.[39] Although scarcely noted heretofore, the contribution of Cambridge to the character of the Georgian movement was decisive. In addition to its massive influence on Marsh, its effect upon Brooke was hardly less; and, indeed, it was on one of Marsh's frequent visits to Cambridge that they met, in January 1907, during Brooke's first year there. In 1908 they planned their second or third meeting to take place at a gathering of the Apostles Society, the select undergraduate company that Marsh had been invited to join — together with Russell and Moore — about fifteen years earlier. According to Hassall, at the beginning of their friendship, before they had begun to address themselves by their Christian names, the transactions of the Apostles Society "were their only common ground."[40] When Marsh, Russell, and Moore had been undergraduate members of the Society, its dominant figure was the philosopher Henry Sidgwick who had played a leading part in the establishment of agnosticism at Cambridge. Elected to the Society in 1856, Sidgwick carried forward its tradition (going back to Tennyson and Hallam in the 1820s) of strenuous thought and discussion, to which he added his dedication to "absolute candour" as the primary obligation in "the pursuit of truth."[41] Sidgwick died in 1900; and when, in 1908, Marsh and Brooke gathered with the Apostles, the reigning figure was Moore. Hassall

---

39. Leading Bloomsburians like E. M. Forster, Desmond MacCarthy, and Raymond Mortimer were, in fact, close friends of Marsh.

40. Hassall, *A Biography of Edward Marsh*, pp. 142-143.

41. Sidgwick remarks of the Apostles' discussions that "No consistency was demanded with opinions previously held — truth as we saw it then and there was what we had to embrace and maintain, and there were no propositions so well established that an Apostle had not the right to deny or question, if he did so sincerely and not from mere love of paradox." See Arthur Sidgwick and Eleanor M. Sidgwick, *Henry Sidgwick: A Memoir* (London, 1906), pp. 29-32, 34-35. Russell has provided this characterization of the Society: "It was a principle in discussion that there were to be no *taboos*, no limitations, nothing considered shocking, no barriers to absolute freedom of speculation." See *The Autobiography of Bertrand Russell: 1872-1914* (London, 1967), p. 69.

notes that Moore's ideas struck Brooke "with the force of a revelation." He cites Brooke's description of Moore as "the greatest living philosopher."[42] Hassall offers this account of what Brooke discovered, inter alia, from his conversations with Moore:

> To know *exactly* what one feels is the prime duty, avoiding all ready-made and traditional wisdom, habitual response or convention, basing one's judgement strictly on the exercise of reason, each man his own severest judge in his own case. Feeling without the check of reason is suspect; general principles of conduct, of course, such as the Victorian sense of duty, are anathema, and religious dogma is not merely untrue but unnecessary.[43]

These were, of course, ideas that Marsh had entertained with Moore a decade earlier, while the philosopher was first engaged in working them out. It was, in fact, only after Brooke's awakening to the presence of Moore in 1908 that he and Marsh became close friends. Their first meeting had apparently made little impression on Marsh, who subsequently described Brooke at this time as cultivating a languishing "decadent" pose, mounting Aubrey Beardsley drawings in his room, and sitting up very late at night in order to rise late, in the approved "aesthetic" manner.[44] But a year or two later, says Marsh, quoting one of Brooke's collegiate contemporaries, "the atmosphere of Cambridge was teaching him to value and to cultivate lucidity of thought and precision of reasoning."[45] Brooke himself carefully distinguished between his

---

42. Hassall, *Rupert Brooke*, pp. 155-156. See also p. 144. At the very head of a fastidiously drawn list of recommended reading that he sent in July 1909 to his cousin Erica Cotterill, Brooke wrote, "Read: *G. E. Moore's Principia Ethica* very slowly & carefully, as you want to think." Geoffrey Keynes, ed., *The Letters of Rupert Brooke* (London, 1968), p. 173. For evidence of Moore's direct influence upon Brooke, see Brooke's "A or B?" a paper read to the Apostles in 1909, in Timothy Rogers, *Rupert Brooke: A Reappraisal and Selection* (London, 1971), pp. 116-121; and his "Notes on Drama and the Nature of Art" (ca. 1910), Christopher Hassall, ed., *The Prose of Rupert Brooke* (London, 1956), pp. 168-175, especially p. 169 where Brooke employs Moore's idea of the "naturalistic fallacy": "The good of plays is not in their being made, or played, or in making you a good citizen. It is in your state of mind *when you watch a play.*" Written in 1911-12 as a Cambridge dissertation, Brooke's *John Webster and the Elizabethan Drama* (London, 1916) provides abundant evidence of his indebtedness to *Principia Ethica*; see the first chapter, in which Brooke's definition of the aesthetic assumptions underlying his study generally follows Moore's language and method in the *Principia.*

43. Hassall, *Rupert Brooke*, p. 155.

44. Marsh, "Memoir," in *Rupert Brooke: The Collected Poems*, p. xxiii.

45. *Ibid.*, p. xxx.

poems written before and after 1908. Indeed, on the appearance of *Poems* (1911), he separated readers who praised the early poems in his "aesthetic" manner from readers like Marsh who praised "the ones I like . . . the ones by *me*, not by a frail pleasant youth of the same name who died in 1908."[46] Apart from Brooke's striking good looks and manifest charm, he and Marsh were drawn together by a shared philosophical tutelage. Separated by more than a decade, they were nevertheless in philosophic, political, and aesthetic accord.

Further, of the first contributors to *Georgian Poetry*, many had either attended Cambridge or had been otherwise linked with it. Robert Trevelyan had moved in the same intellectual circle as had Marsh at Cambridge. Sturge Moore was G. E. Moore's brother. Harold Monro had come down from Cambridge in 1901. James Elroy Flecker had come to Cambridge for advanced studies in Oriental languages, following his undergraduate career at Oxford, and met Brooke there in 1908. Indeed, Flecker's biographer has noted that "Cambridge made him a Liberal, even an enthusiastic Liberal."[47] D. H. Lawrence had been introduced to Cambridge by Bertrand Russell; and, although predictably repelled by its prevailing rationalism, he was — according to J. M. Keynes — very much attracted to it.[48] Marsh's invitation to A. E. Housman to appear in the first volume of *Georgian Poetry* was another instance of the way in which Cambridge served as its catalyst, for he had been elected Kennedy Professor of Latin at Cambridge in 1911.[49] Finally, while John Squire was not formally linked with *Georgian Poetry* until his inclusion in the third volume, his importance to the second stage of the movement makes it worth noting that — three years before Brooke — he too came down from Cambridge.[50]

46. G. Keynes, *The Letters of Rupert Brooke*, pp. 326-327. Hassall notes, "The poet who died in 1908 (I would put the date at least a year later) was of course the spiritual offspring of Dowson" (*The Prose of Rupert Brooke*, p. xxviii).

47. Douglas Goldring, *James Elroy Flecker* (London, 1922), p. 40.

48. J. M. Keynes, *Two Memoirs*, pp. 79-80.

49. Housman politely declined on the grounds that he did not "really belong" to Marsh's "new era" and that he had written no poems during 1911-12, the dates of composition to which contributors were presumably restricted. But he proposed that Marsh include Chesterton's "Ballad of the White Horse." Letter from A.E. Housman to Edward Marsh, dated October 1, 1912, in the Berg Collection of the New York Public Library.

50. Squire's biographer observes that, whereas at his preparatory school "he had been an unhesitating conformist, at Cambridge he began to develop new and individual tastes and opinions." See Patrick Howarth, *Squire: "Most Generous of Men"* (London, 1963), p. 28.

It is, therefore, hardly sufficient to say of Marsh and Brooke that "their common enthusiasm was the foundation of *Georgian Poetry*."[51] When a loose association of poets commenced to take shape around Marsh and Brooke in 1911 and 1912,[52] it was composed of men who were either products of Cambridge liberalism or nonacademic independents like Wilfrid Gibson, W. H. Davies, Lascelles Abercrombie, Gordon Bottomley, and D. H. Lawrence. Although widely dispersed and variously occupied, they were all possessed by a desire to report experience faithfully; they were all unwilling to subordinate the writing of poetry to any other purpose. Their liberal, independent spirit was fully evident in their unconcern for authority. Their general orientation did not incline them to dwell upon the achievement of a group discipline, to formulate a manifesto. Indeed, their very stance militated against consolidation into a "movement." Consequently, the Georgians are most easily defined through reference to what they were against. For example, the notion that Georgian poetics consisted of negations or prohibitions is stressed by Herbert Palmer. Of the fourteen principles of early Georgian poetry listed by Palmer, no less than thirteen are negative admonitions.[53]

51. Hassall, *A Biography of Edward Marsh*, p. 178.

52. Marsh and Harold Monro, for example, met when a mutual acquaintance suggested to Marsh that his admiration of Brooke's poetry might reach a wider circle through the *Poetry Review*, which Monro was editing. This acquaintance carried to Monro the information that Marsh would willingly review Brooke's first book of poems. Marsh and Monro (the future editor and publisher of *Georgian Poetry*) were thus thrown together, early in 1912, by their shared interest in the work of Brooke. See Hassall, *A Biography of Edward Marsh*, pp. 181-182. In the same casual fashion, friends of Brooke — like Flecker — were brought to the attention of Marsh; and friends of Marsh — like Gibson and de la Mare — were brought to the attention of Brooke. See, for example, John Sherwood, *No Golden Journey: A Biography of James Elroy Flecker* (London, 1973), pp. 156-157.

53. Herbert Palmer, *Post-Victorian Poetry* (London, 1938), pp. 76-78. As Graves and Riding put it, the "general recommendations" and "counsels" of the Georgians "resulted in a poetry that could rather be praised for what it was not than for what it was." See Laura Riding and Robert Graves, *A Survey of Modernist Poetry* (London, 1927), pp. 118-119.

3

THE CHARACTER OF
GEORGIAN OPPOSITION

The Georgians shared, most obviously, a distaste for the public manner — the empty rhetoric — of much late Victorian "improving" poetry (as represented, for example, in the work of Sir William Watson and Alfred Noyes). And, as in the case of Brooke's development, they found the sweetly narcissistic amorality of the Decadents an unsatisfactory alternative.[1] English poetry seemed clearly to have fallen upon hard times, that is, a period of very low energy, and to have fallen into the wrong hands. J. M. Cohen offers this account of the state of English poetry in the last decade of the nineteenth century and the first decade of the twentieth:

> A cycle appeared to be running out in bombast, preciosity or smug provincialism. The most appealing poets were those who . . . deliberately constricted their vision to their own region and their favourite books. Ranging thoughts were deliberately called home. . . . Better this than the grandiose emptiness of Francis Thompson at his most banal, loud with echoes of all the poets who had gone before him. . . . In such poetry, built up of reminiscences from Shakespeare, Shelley, Coleridge and Patmore, or in the even flatter pastiche of Stephen Phillips and William Watson, the commonplaces of the Renaissance tradition received their final twist of bathos; the motifs of heroism and romantic love, of rejoicing with the rebirth of Nature in Spring and grief at her death in Autumn, of the relation between a god that could be drawn in man's image and a man who faced the world in the confidence that he was captain of his own soul, were no longer capable of inspiring even passably good poems. First the poet and

---

1. Samuel C. Chew asserts that to the extent the Georgians "shared a common program, it was an unexcited protest against the meretricious passion of the 'Decadents' and against the stylistic flaccidity and lassitude of late-nineteenth-century verse" (*A Literary History of England*, ed. Albert C. Baugh [New York, 1948], p. 1579).

then the sensitive public had come to realize that there was a hollowness at the heart of things. The first reaction to this discovery was the so-called 'Decadent' movement of the nineties, but it was impossible to make a new poetry only out of tears.[2]

Speaking of writers who merely mime the attitudes and verbal gestures of their distinguished predecessors, J. I. M. Stewart says, "If one wants to see this particular sort of wrongness in chemical purity one has to turn to William Watson."[3] In poems like his "Ode on the Day of the Coronation of King Edward VII," Watson revealed his eagerness to carry on the tradition of the public poet, the national bard, which the Victorians' veneration of Wordsworth, Tennyson, and Browning had served to magnify:

> Sire, we have looked on many and mighty things
> In these eight hundred summers of renown
> Since the Gold Dragon of the Wessex Kings
> On Hastings field went down. . . .[4]

In his manifest pride in the empire, in his proclaimed sense of the historical destiny of the British people, Watson stood with Kipling, Noyes, and Sir Henry Newbolt. His patriotism, like theirs, extended easily into intense nativism and xenophobia (see "Home-Rootedness"), into literary chauvinism (see "On Exaggerated Deference to Foreign Literary Opinion"), and into the assertion of conventional religious views (see "The Unknown God," "To One Who Had Written in Derision of the Belief in Immortality," and "Sacrifice").[5] This was the sort of poetry, albeit earlier practiced by the great Romantics and Victorians with freshness and power, that had brought poets into close harmony with a large popular

2. J. M. Cohen, *Poetry of This Age* (Philadelphia, 1962), pp. 33-34.

3. J. I. M. Stewart, *Eight Modern Writers* (Oxford, 1963), p. 4.

4. William Watson, *The Poems of William Watson* (London, 1905), II, 95. The typical reader of poetry, according to Watson, "is not so tired of the great writers of the past as to resent any natural and inherited resemblance to them in their successors. Rather is he pleased to see the ancient ancestral lineaments reappear, and to think that the noble tradition in which he was nurtured is being nobly perpetuated." William Watson, "The Poet's Place in the Scheme of Life," in *The Muse in Exile* (London, 1913), p. 25. Watson maintained that "The true function of the poet to-day is to keep fresh within us our often flagging sense of life's greatness and grandeur" and that the "crowning grace" of poetry is "harmonious utterance" (pp. 29, 30).

5. For an excellent discussion of the political and aesthetic orientation of these Conservative or Imperialist poets whom the Georgians repudiated, see C. K. Stead, *The New Poetic* (London, 1964), pp. 67-79.

audience; and it continued to do so. Watson was widely esteemed a great poet; and Newbolt's vigorous patriotism and espousal of the "solid" English values won him great public acceptance. His first book of poems, *Admirals All* (1897), had by 1912 run through thirty printings.[6] Indeed, according to Herbert Palmer, "one of his [Newbolt's] reviewers said of his relationship to his public that he was 'in danger of confusing it with a public meeting,' meaning, I suppose, that mere rhetoric was triumphing over song."[7] But this was precisely the risk assumed by even the most eminent Victorians. Edith Batho and Bonamy Dobrée state that one of the characteristics of Victorian poetry is "the sense poets felt that they had an immediate mission, ought to utter a message." They add that Victorian readers apparently did not care "whether poetry was present or not, so long as they got the doctrine, the revelation, or the interpretation."[8] Poetic and public interests blurred: the "successful" poet increasingly — if more emptily — demonstrated his natural or learned responsiveness to the popular desiderata of literary achievement.[9]

If the late Victorian poets seemed to have carried their concern for literary decorum and social piety to an ossified extreme, it was because so many details of modern life were already present. By 1910, airplanes, psychoanalysis, postimpressionist painting, and the Labor Party were already part of the scene; but the forms of established authority appeared to take no notice of them, and thus traditional authority appeared all the more foolishly restrictive and irrelevant. The early works of E. M. Forster, Virginia Woolf, D. H. Lawrence, James Joyce, Ezra Pound, and T. S. Eliot were written during the laureateship of Alfred Austin. By 1910, a direct confrontation between the Old and the New, in nearly every sphere of English life, was well under way. The coronation of George V in 1910 provided an obvious name for the new spirits

6. Herbert Palmer, *Post-Victorian Poetry* (London, 1938), p. 38.

7. *Ibid.*, p. 43.

8. Edith C. Batho and Bonamy Dobrée, *The Victorians and After* (London, 1950), p. 41.

9. For an incisive account of the public audience for literature in the first decade of this century, see Stead, *The New Poetic*, chap. 3 (esp. pp. 45-52). See also Harold Monro's satiric portrait of the contemporary poetic opportunist in *Some Contemporary Poets* (London, 1920), p. 14; and Ezra Pound's "Mr. Nixon" (from *Hugh Selwyn Mauberley*) in *Personae: Collected Shorter Poems of Ezra Pound* (London, 1952), pp. 203-204.

gathering force in English society, in general, and in English poetry in particular. In a letter to Blanche Jennings, dated July 17, 1908, D. H. Lawrence expressed the negative mood out of which *Georgian Poetry* was born:

> Poetry now-a-days seems to be a sort of plaster-cast craze, scraps sweetly moulded in easy Plaster of Paris sentiment. Nobody chips verses earnestly out of the living rock of his own feeling. . . . Before everything I like sincerity, and a quickening spontaneous emotion.[10]

When eloquence is no longer eloquent of anything that cuts deeply into human experience, it becomes rhetoric: the competent manipulation of tested verbal gestures. Traditionalists like Sir William Watson and Alfred Noyes were thus regarded as rhetoricians by Marsh, Brooke, and their circle, who perceived with displeasure that genuine poetry had been counterfeited, had been replaced with formulas that ensured public approval. The Georgians, in other words, questioned the honesty of the relationship — as "Victorianly" conceived — between the poet, his subject matter, and his audience. That Watson, Newbolt, Kipling, Noyes, and Stephen Phillips could be so generally acclaimed seemed to the Georgians both an indication that public standards of poetry were to be either corrected or ignored and a sign of the misfeasance of these then regnant poets.

Thus, far from being uncritically conservative, the Georgians were avowedly and comprehensively anti-Victorian. Influenced directly and indirectly by Moore and Russell, they were wary of simplistically grandiose metaphysical and ethical assumptions. A virtually uniform agnosticism contributed heavily to their disaffection from the doctrinaire quality of much Victorian religious verse, with its initial hesitancies the unvarying prelude to its climactic certitude.[11] In a comment on a humorous sonnet he

10. Harry T. Moore, ed., *The Collected Letters of D. H. Lawrence* (New York, 1962), I, 21.

11. H. N. Fairchild notes that "the main body of Georgian nature poetry ignores the existence of even the most shadowy transcendent deity" (*Religious Trends in English Poetry* [New York, 1962], V, 364). Christopher Hassall reports, "If it were possible for a man to be temperamentally incapable of any kind of transcendental belief Eddie Marsh was he" (*A Biography of Edward Marsh* [New York, 1959], p. 46). In a letter to a fellow Fabian, F. H. Keeling, expressing mild dissent from Keeling's pessimism, Brooke

sent to Violet Asquith, Brooke ironized his contempt for "uplift" poetry:

> Oh, dear! I suppose it ought to end on the Higher Note, the Wider Outlook. Poetry has to, they tell me. You may caress details all the main part of the poem, but at last you have to open the window — turn to God, or Earth, or Eternity, or any of the Grand Old Endings. It gives Uplift. . . . And that's so essential. (Did you ever notice how the Browning family's poems *all* refer suddenly to God in the last line. It's laughable if you read through them in that way. "What if that friend happened to be — God?", "What comes next — Is it God?", "And with God be the rest," "And if God choose, I shall but love thee better after Death" — etc. etc. I forget them all, now. It shows what the Victorians were.)[12]

Deeply attentive to Hardy and Samuel Butler, they found there additional support for their disposition to question easy assertions of the idea of immortality and an ingenuous faith in the certainty of progress. They learned from Hardy and Butler to view men as suffering creatures, both naturally and cosmically oppressed. Uniformly Liberals and Fabians, they sharply rejected the patriotic championing of the English social and economic systems that bulked so large in the verse of the late Victorian establishment.[13]

---

wrote, "Do not leap or turn pale at the word Mysticism. I do not mean any religious thing, or any form of belief. I still burn and torture Christians daily. It is merely the *feeling* — or a kindred one — which underlay the mysticism of the wicked Mystics. Only I refuse to be cheated by the *feeling* into any kind of *belief*" (Geoffrey Keynes, ed., *The Letters of Rupert Brooke* [London, 1968], p. 258). Douglas Goldring states that Flecker was "fond of saying that he was an agnostic" (*James Elroy Flecker* [London, 1922], p. 145). And Lawrence certainly shared the Georgians' patronizing view of religion: "The secret of religion is, I think, that one can remain a child without losing any of one's importance. As a matter of fact, most folks are afraid to grow up; that's why they defer it so long. Real independence and self-responsibility are terrifying to the majority" (letter to Blanche Jennings, dated July 17, 1908, in Moore, ed., *The Collected Letters of D. H. Lawrence*, I, 19).

12. Keynes, ed., *The Letters of Rupert Brooke*, pp. 541-542.

13. See Robert H. Ross, *The Georgian Revolt, 1910-1922* (Carbondale, Ill. 1965), p. 12. The fall of the Conservative or Unionist government in 1905 and the resounding triumph of the Liberal-Labor coalition in the general election of 1906, with the ensuing Campbell-Bannerman and Asquith governments, are likely to have fortified the conviction of the Marsh group in 1911 and 1912 that Victorianism was in retreat. Marsh was himself a Liberal who served Winston Churchill, then one of the most promising of the Liberal politicians. "Monro came down from Cambridge in 1901 a fervent Fabian Socialist" (Ross, p. 58). Early in 1906, Squire participated in the founding of a Fabian society at Cambridge; and he was instrumental in linking the Cambridge Fabians with the local branch of the Independent Labor Party (see Patrick Howarth, *Squire: "Most Generous of Men"* [London, 1963], p. 40). Squire stood for Parliament first as a Labor

The Georgians were in protest against forms of thought and expression — encrusted and embellished — within which the essential truths of human experience could not be told, simply and directly, but which committed the poet, rather, to the utterance of those pronouncements that the public wished to hear.

The patent hostility of the early Georgians to what they understood to be the Victorian poetic tradition, with particular reference to its surviving remnant, is now more evident than heretofore. It is true that Herbert Palmer had remarked in 1938 the Georgians' particular criticism of Kipling's imperialist attitude, and he had observed that Stephen Phillips was one of the "accepted" poets early in this century "until the Georgians pushed him completely out of the ring."[14] But it is the recent biographical and critical studies of Hassall, Ross, and Stead that have made fully explicit the anti-Victorianism of the Georgians. In his account of the views that Brooke held by 1908, Hassall reports, "The liquidation of Victorianism . . . was now an intellectual passion and his mission in life."[15] And in his description of the conversation between Marsh and Brooke in which *Georgian Poetry* was conceived, Hassall says, "They believed that Victorianism in literature was gone for good and that a new era had begun."[16] Monro fortified his dissent from Marsh's wish to include in the third volume of *Georgian Poetry* an elegy by his old friend Maurice Baring with the charge that its "Victorian language and images" disqualified it as Georgian.[17] According to Hassall, again,

---

and then as a Liberal candidate; and, more important, he first achieved literary recognition as the literary editor of the *New Statesman,* which had been established as an organ of Fabian opinion. Marsh tells us that Brooke "had been the chief advocate of the Labour Party at Rugby; and at King's he joined various societies, political and intellectual, mostly more or less revolutionary — the University Fabian Society, of which he became President for the year 1909-10" (Edward Marsh, ed., *Rupert Brooke: The Collected Poems* [London, 1918], p. xxvii). And when Flecker met Brooke at Cambridge, he too joined the Fabians (Goldring, *James Elroy Flecker*, p. 39). Indeed, Flecker felt that poetry flourished during periods of intense political commitment, and that poets came alive in responding to a climate of political strife and revolution (*ibid.*, pp. 41-42). All this merits consideration in relation to the conventional depiction of the Georgians as tame, escapist poets.

14. Palmer, *Post-Victorian Poetry*, pp. 47, 61. See also p. 76, where Palmer notes that the early Georgian poets made "a definite attempt to break away from the Tennysonian tradition, from Tennysonian influences. . . ." "This new poetry," Palmer adds, "constituted a definite break with nearly everything known as 'Victorian.' "

15. Christopher Hassall, *Rupert Brooke* (London, 1964), p. 157.

16. Hassall, *A Biography of Edward Marsh*, p. 189.

17. *Ibid.*, p. 421.

Lascelles Abercrombie — at the time of the first appearance of *Georgian Poetry* — "believed that the Georgians had broken away completely from Victorianism in manner as well as matter."[18]

Although it has been usual to think of the Georgians as dedicated to large sales of their books, they were quite honestly surprised by the magnitude of the public response to them. In fact, they regarded their anthologies as a kind of counterstatement to the work of the celebrated late Victorians whose sales were often immense, at least by contemporary standards. For example, wryly addressing himself to Alfred Noyes's great commercial successes, Marsh composed this pun in a letter to Edmund Blunden:

> I am pleased to know that whereas in the Ancient Mariner "still the sails made on their pleasant noise till noon" it is now Noyes who still makes on his pleasant sales till closing time.[19]

Robert Ross — using the term "Georgian," in his introductory chapters, to refer to the generalized revival of poetry in the early twentieth century as well as, more specifically, to the Marsh circle — stresses heavily in both applications of the term the anti-Victorianism of the Georgians.[20]   And C. K. Stead is specially concerned to remind us that the young Georgians (by whom he means the original Marsh circle), far from being reactionary, were generally regarded in 1912 as "dangerous literary revolutionaries." He adds that Marsh himself was at this time "generally regarded as a daring innovator."[21]   The late Victorians replied with suitable indignation to the attacks and alternative poetic mode of the Georgians. William Watson, for example, accused them of being averse to smoothness, of being thoroughly dedicated to the achievement of cacophonous effects in their poetry, and thus of doing a profound disservice to poetry by writing in a style that suggested contempt for the traditional uses of prosody and rhetoric:

18. *Ibid.*, p. 681.
19. Quoted in Hassall, *A Biography of Edward Marsh*, p. 522.
20. Ross, *The Georgian Revolt*, pp. 20-21, 120.
21. Stead, *The New Poetic*, p. 57. Robert Graves, perhaps mindful of the picture of Marsh and his Georgians that had taken form since the twenties, reminisced thus in a memorial volume for Marsh: "It is nice to remember that Eddie was once a daring innovator . . ." (Christopher Hassall and Denis Mathews, comps., *Eddie Marsh: Sketches for a Composite Literary Portrait of Sir Edward Marsh* [London, 1953], p. 25).

Certain of our Georgian singers, and even one or two poets whose roots go down into late-Victorian antiquity, are so haunted by a dread of smoothness that they have very nearly erected cacophony into a cult. They pursue it as an end in itself laudable. . . .

And here I should greatly like to pause, and, if it be possible, rescue this word *rhetoric* from the evil habits into which it has latterly fallen by no innate fault of its own. This once quite honourable word is now become a term of rank abuse, a portable handy missile to be heaved at any obnoxious man of verse who has not founded himself altogether on "Mary had a little lamb," or the "Songs of Innocence," or other lyrism similarly untainted with the vices of the rhetorician.[22]

In commencing thus to define the Georgian poetic first through reference to what it opposed, in stressing initially recognition of the Georgians as reformist poets in rebellion against both Victorian doctrinizing and Decadence, one is able to discern the basis for the easy fraternity that existed between the Hulme-Pound circle and Marsh's Georgians from 1911 to about 1913.[23] They possessed common enemies, and their criticisms of these shared enemies were often indistinguishable. Consequently, during this period a kind of "popular front" or coalition (not unlike that between Liberals and Laborites) existed among the opponents of the late Victorians. Robert Ross has properly noted that the common ground of Marsh's Georgians and the "Leftist" or Modernist poets was their anti-Victorianism.[24] Both Georgian and Imagist recoiled from Victorian decorum and solemnity, from turgid and ornate poetic diction, and from enervated sensualism. The popular poetry of this time, as for example C. K. Stead has described it,[25] was mutually unacceptable to Marsh and Pound.

22. William Watson, *Pencraft: A Plea for the Older Ways* (London, 1916), pp. 50, 58. It may also be noted here that Hassall, speaking of the literary situation in July 1914, has observed, "For the present to be Georgian was, oddly enough, to be thought obscure" (*A Biography of Edward Marsh*, p. 289).

23. See Alun R. Jones, *The Life and Opinions of T. E. Hulme* (Boston, 1960), pp. 35-36, 88-89, 95, 99-101.

24. Ross, *The Georgian Revolt*, p. 120. See, for example, Pound's essay on Lionel Johnson (1915): "for Milton and Victorianism and for the softness of the 'nineties' I have different degrees of antipathy or even contempt." The essay is reprinted in T. S. Eliot, ed., *Literary Essays of Ezra Pound* (London, 1954), p. 362.

25. Stead, *The New Poetic*, p. 49.

Thus, they found themselves briefly in essential accord as to the poetic habits and mannerisms that were to be discarded.

In 1912 and 1913, Marsh saw T. E. Hulme often; he attended his lectures and discussion evenings, and in his company he went to hear Pound lecture and read his poems. Together friends of Hulme, Marsh and Pound were at this time on decidedly good terms.[26] Indeed, when — on September 19, 1912 — Marsh and Brooke first discussed the desirability of issuing an anthology of the new poetry, they included Ezra Pound among their prospective contributors.[27] In a letter of January 22, 1913, in which he adverts to his "friend Marsh," Flecker also refers collectively to "these Masefields . . . Gibsons, Pounds, Abercrombies."[28] Pound, on his part, recommended W. H. Davies's poems to Harriet Monroe and apparently attempted to secure several of them for publication in *Poetry.*[29] And, significantly, Harold Monro's Poetry Bookshop was the publisher of both *Georgian Poetry* and Pound's anthology *Des Imagistes.*

Moreover, some of the proposals and practices of the Imagist circle appeared thoroughly consistent with those of the Georgians. Pound's notion at this time that the achievement of truth and beauty in poetry necessitated the poet's withdrawal from public posturing, that is, the subordination or extinction of his personality in the interest of an absolute dedication to his craft, and his consequent abandonment of the rhetorical formulas that ensured popular approval, seemed entirely compatible with the orientation of the Marsh group. In "The Serious Artist" (1913) Pound admonishes the poet not to allow his concern for the expectations of his readers to make him a liar:

> If an artist falsifies his report as to the nature of man, as to his own nature, as to the nature of his ideal of the perfect, as to the nature of his ideal of this, that or the other, of god, if god exist, of the life force, of the nature of good and evil, if good and evil exist, of the force with which he believes or disbelieves this, that or the other, of the degree in which he suffers or is made glad; if

26. Hassall, *A Biography of Edward Marsh,* p. 193.
27. *Ibid.*, p. 189. For an account of the circumstances behind Pound's absence from the first volume of *Georgian Poetry*, see p. 193.
28. Quoted in Goldring, *James Elroy Flecker*, pp. 74-75.
29. See D. D. Paige, ed., *The Letters of Ezra Pound* (New York, 1950), p. 81.

the artist falsifies his reports on these matters or on any other matter in order that he may conform to the taste of his time, to the proprieties of a sovereign, to the conveniences of a preconceived code of ethics, then that artist lies. If he lies out of deliberate will to lie, if he lies out of carelessness, out of laziness, out of cowardice, out of any sort of negligence whatsoever, he nevertheless lies and he should be punished or despised in proportion to the seriousness of his offence.[30]

Speaking of beauty in art, Pound carefully differentiates his conception from the conventional view:

> I am not now speaking of shams. I mean beauty, not slither, not sentimentalizing about beauty, not telling people that beauty is the proper and respectable thing.[31]

Artistic disinterestedness, a reluctance on the artist's part to consider his own or the reader's advantage in the execution of his artistic endeavors, contributes importantly to an impersonal theory of literature. Pound declares that "it is not the artist's place to ask you to learn, or to defend his particular works of art, or to insist on your reading his books. Any artist who wants your particular admiration is, by just so much, the less artist." He adds, "The desire to stand on the stage, the desire of plaudits has nothing to do with serious art."[32] And he credits the major poets with "a sort of modesty, a sort of unselfishness."[33]

Thus, with the Georgians, Pound regarded popular poets like William Watson as rhetoricians rather than poets, as facile imitators and crowd pleasers. In 1915, Pound described Watson as "capable of deceiving you for a time by his airs of being the true master instead of a very serious and accomplished substitute."

30. Eliot, ed., *Literary Essays of Ezra Pound*, pp. 43-44.

31. *Ibid.*, p. 45.

32. *Ibid.*, pp. 46-47.

33. *Ibid.*, p. 49. This view of Pound's — shared with, if not indeed derived from, T.E. Hulme — found its most celebrated expression in T. S. Eliot's "Tradition and the Individual Talent" (1919), in which Eliot refers specifically to an "impersonal theory of poetry." In this essay he states what both early Georgians and Imagists would have fully endorsed: "Poetry is not a turning loose of emotion, but an escape from emotion; it is not the expression of personality, but an escape from personality." In his assertion that "the progress of an artist is . . . a continual extinction of personality," Eliot was carrying forward the effort of early Georgians and Imagists alike to place both the poet and the public back into a proper relationship with the poem. See T. S. Eliot, *The Sacred Wood* (London, 1920), pp. 53, 58.

Watson, Pound continues, "has *worked at poetry*, and has made himself a sonorous *orator*, a fine declaimer, a dexterous manager of words."[34]   Again, with the Georgians, Pound admired those older English poets who were neither public flatterers nor entertainers. Speaking in 1916 of the Old English poem "The Seafarer," Pound says that these lines "were made for no man's entertainment, but because a man believing in silence found himself unable to withhold himself from speaking." Pound concludes his sharp attack upon the view that poetry is meant to serve the public by noting of "The Seafarer" and "The Wanderer" that "such poems are not made for afterdinner speakers."[35]

With Marsh's Georgians, the early Imagists repudiated abstract language. Together, they attempted to cultivate a poetic diction that was "hard," precise, objective, clear. "The serious artist," said Pound in 1913, "is scientific in that he presents the image of his desire, of his hate, of his indifference as precisely that, as precisely the image of his own desire, hate or indifference. The more precise his record the more lasting and unassailable his work of art."[36] Pound adds, "Good writing is writing that is perfectly controlled, the writer says just what he means. He says it with complete clarity and simplicity."[37]   Anxious to keep the central principles of Imagism — as they had been formulated by Hulme and others before 1910 — quite distinct from the heterogeneous movement, calling itself Imagism, over which by 1914 Amy Lowell was presiding, Pound wrote Miss Lowell on August 1, 1914, that he would like Imagism "to stand for hard light, clear edges." Little more than a week later, he wrote her again to protest the use of "Imagism" as a title for the anthology of miscellaneous free verse poetry she was assembling. Pound feared that some of the poets she had included did not even understand what he meant by Imagism. Accordingly, he wrote, "I should, as I have said, like to keep the term associated with a certain clarity and intensity."[38] Finally, there is Pound's letter to Harriet Monroe in January 1915, in which he begins with the now familiar aphorism that "Poetry

34. Eliot, ed., *Literary Essays of Ezra Pound*, p. 364.
35. *Ibid.*, pp. 64-65.
36. *Ibid.*, p. 46.
37. *Ibid.*, p. 50.
38. Paige, ed., *The Letters of Ezra Pound*, pp. 38, 39.

must be *as well written as prose,"* a judgment upon poetic language fully acceptable to Marsh, whose views on this subject had
been heavily influenced by his favorite teacher at Cambridge, the
distinguished classicist and Dryden scholar Arthur W. Verrall.
Pound's letter to Miss Monroe elaborates the early Imagist conception of the proper language of poetry:

> Its language must be a fine language, departing in no way from
> speech save by a heightened intensity (i.e. simplicity). There must
> be no book words, no periphrases, no inversions.

.   .   .   .

> There must be no cliches, set phrases, stereotyped journalese.
> The only escape from such is by precision, a result of con-
> centrated attention to what is writing. The test of a writer is his
> ability for such concentration AND for his power to stay con-
> centrated till he gets to the end of his poem, whether it is two
> lines or two hundred.
>
> Objectivity and again objectivity, and expression: no hindside-
> beforeness, no straddled adjectives (as "addled mosses dank"), no
> Tennysonianness of speech; nothing — nothing that you couldn't,
> in some circumstance, in the stress of some emotion, actually say.
> Every literaryism, every book word, fritters away a scrap of the
> reader's patience, a scrap of his sense of your sincerity. When one
> really feels and thinks, one stammers with simple speech; it is
> only in the flurry, the shallow frothy excitement of writing, or
> the inebriety of a metre, that one falls into the easy — oh, how
> easy! — speech of books and poems that one has read.[39]

In their common desire to recall poetry to the genuine truths of
human experience, both the early Georgians and the early Imagists
were quite willing to restrict radically the subject matter of poetry
to what could be known by the poet directly and stated accurately. Both groups were, moreover, opposed to the use of poetry for
doctrinizing, for conveying moral or political messages. Consequently, the disposition of Marsh's Georgians to reduce the scope
of poetry by severely pruning poetic diction and banishing doc-
trinal content was virtually identical with that of the Imagists who
were guided by the poetics of T. E. Hulme. It is, therefore, hardly

39. *Ibid.*, pp. 48-49.

surprising that both the Georgians and the Imagists have been criticized for their supposed diminishing of poetry from Romantic sublimity and Victorian grandeur to trivial, indeed Lilliputian, proportions. The following quite conventional appraisal of the Imagists is literally indistinguishable from one commonly made of the Georgians:

> Up to a point the Imagist prospectus was unexceptionable; their insistence on precision, conciseness, and clarity was all to the good; but by limiting poetry to the image they condemned themselves to carving cherry-stones.[40]

One has only to substitute the notion of a poetry limited to the countryside for that of a poetry limited to the image to perceive a momentary blurring of these two poetic schools, whose differences were in fact profound.

In a letter to Brooke of June 22, 1913, Marsh reported "the first rumours of opposition to Georgian Poetry":

> Wilfrid [Gibson] tells me there's a movement for a "Post-Georgian" anthology, of the Pound-Flint-Hulme school, who don't like being out of G. P. but I don't think it will come off. [41]

At about this time, as his own letters reveal,[42] Pound began to express a pronounced dissatisfaction with the "literary method" of Abercrombie and Brooke. Pound's poem "Our Contemporaries" is obviously aimed at Brooke, and suggests that his poetry is remote from life — from true intensity of feeling — and, moreover, that it is mechanically literary, in the manner of the late Victorians:

> When the Taihaitian princess
> Heard that he had decided,
> She rushed out into the sunlight and swarmed up a
>   cocoanut palm tree,
>
> But he returned to this island
> And wrote ninety Petrarchan sonnets.[43]

40. Herbert J. C. Grierson and J. C. Smith, *A Critical History of English Poetry* (London, 1956), p. 500.
41. Quoted in Hassall, *A Biography of Edward Marsh*, p. 229.
42. Paige, ed., *The Letters of Ezra Pound*, pp. 12, 64, 66.
43. Pound, *Personae*, p. 129. The poem originally appeared in July 1915, in the second number of *Blast*.

Indeed, in the "Note" that accompanies the poem, Pound specifically identifies the style of the first Georgian anthology as Victorian. Brooke, for his part, had as early as December 1909 expressed his reservations concerning Pound's poetic mannerisms and his "dangerous" addiction to free verse.[44] And Marsh, noting that Pound had "repeatedly lifted up his horn against the poets who claim my allegiance," questioned Pound's "artistic seriousness" and, by implication, his intellectual honesty.[45]

Robert Ross correctly observes that "the really violent battles of the era raged between the poets of the Center and the Left."[46] That is, once the Marsh group and the several Modernist groups — loosely united by a reformist impulse — had made a common cause of dispatching the Victorian remnant, their "popular front" split on the fundamental issue of whether traditional English poetic standards were to be corrected or replaced by new standards. In the swelling debate arising from this split, Imagists, Futurists, and Vorticists became convinced that Marsh's Georgians were in reality "no more than the last faint re-echo of the Great Tradition."[47] And Marsh's Georgians concluded that the Modernists had overreacted against the poetry of the preceding centuries and were, in consequence, introducing new distortions into the practice of poetry.[48]

The emphasis placed by the Modernists upon the necessity of either reapplying poetic traditions or breaking with them entirely may be best understood in relation to their view of contemporary reality. They regarded the modern world as having undergone so pervasive a change that a new sensibility had taken form. They felt the present so altered from the past, and in many ways so unprecedented, that it imposed upon the poet new experiences and ideas that compelled artistic innovation as a condition of honest expression. They recognized a new reality; and they called, accordingly, for a new art. The Futurists, who were dramatically

---

44. Christopher Hassall, ed., *The Prose of Rupert Brooke* (London, 1956), pp. 111-112.

45. Edward Marsh, *A Number of People* (New York, 1939), pp. 328-329.

46. Ross, *The Georgian Revolt*, p. 23.

47. Monro, *Some Contemporary Poets*, p. 25.

48. This conflict arrived at its most warlike state in the rancorous exchanges between the Sitwells and John Squire from 1918 to about 1924. It was in this later, more polemical context that Georgian poetry — or, more properly, Neo-Georgian poetry — acquired much of its unfortunate reputation.

represented in England by Marinetti, perhaps held this view in its most extreme form; but it was virtually axiomatic among all the Modernists. As Spender puts it, they were "recognizers" who set out deliberately "to invent a new literature as the result of their feeling that our age is in many respects unprecedented, and outside all the conventions of past literature and art."[49] A yet more solipsistic version of this motive underlying Modernism has been provided by Elizabeth Drew:

> Starting from the theory of Relativity, the group of poets who have been named "modernist" points out that all human experience at any given moment is relative to the person who experiences it, and to the particular environment in which it takes place. It is, in fact, unique. It is made up of the relationship of a unique personality with unique circumstances in place and time. This isolation of every mood and moment, this inexorable procession of insecure and fleeting impressions, this shifting, indefinite interplay of elements and dimensions is human life. And the "modernist" poet feels that a conception of life as anything so impermanent as this cannot possibly be suggested by any direct creative methods. He feels that there are no such things as the eternal and unchanging elements in human nature and human experience; that it is only individuals of blunted perceptions and reactions who can live or write by such empty generalizations; that it is impossible to present *his* consciousness of existence in the outworn terms of past approaches to existence, and that he must evolve an entirely new technique to express the unique character of his response.[50]

In opposing this view, Marsh and his Georgians were not flying from reality or protesting against change. Nor were they dully indifferent to ideas. They perceived social and psychological change, but did not find it absolute or sufficiently pervasive to constitute a severe discontinuity with the past. Further, they did not regard art as properly concerned with those levels of thought and experience that are most affected by historical change. Thus, the Georgians saw no need to construct a new poetic, when it was possible — chiefly by example — to purge the old of its errors in practice. They saw no occasion to abandon completely the reading

49. Stephen Spender, *The Struggle of the Modern* (London, 1963), p. x.
50. Elizabeth Drew, *Discovering Poetry* (New York, 1962), p. 71. This book originally appeared in 1933.

public, when it was possible to reestablish the proper distance and relationship between the poet and his audience.[51] Not timidity but an aversion to any distortion – whether from the Left or the Right – of the special function of poetry kept them in the center, where they felt they could deal most honestly and truthfully with those quintessential features of human experience that only art can adequately apprehend. The Georgians were not disposed to concede the relevance of the historical continuum to the writing of genuine poetry; instead, they wrote as though all the "true" poets of the past were their contemporaries. Marsh would indubitably have acquiesced in his friend Forster's insistence that the English novelists are most accurately visualized as "all writing their novels simultaneously" while "seated together" in a circular room. And he would similarly have subscribed to Forster's dictum, "All through history writers while writing have felt more or less the same."[52] From this vantage point, the Georgians regarded the radical linguistic experimentation of the Modernists as, at best, unnecessary and, at worst, absurdly meaningless. Marsh's distress at the formlessness and imprecision of Modernist poetry never abated. In 1942, for example, he wrote thus to Sassoon:

> I woke up the other day from a dream in which I had been reading some modern poet, I don't know who, and found myself saying, "It seems as if a vocabulary had been wandering over the page and at a signal given each word had sat down wherever it happened to be."[53]

51. Stead points out that the Georgians "never adopted the attitude which Pound and the Imagists found to be essential if they were to remain free of hampering influences – the attitude which insisted 'the public can go to the devil.' Theirs was an attempt to educate public taste rather than to dismiss the reading public as too degenerate in taste to deserve consideration" (*The New Poetic*, p. 57). Cf. Paige, ed., *The Letters of Ezra Pound*, p. 48.

52. E. M. Forster, *Aspects of the Novel* (New York, 1927), pp. 21, 38-39.

53. Quoted in Hassall, *A Biography of Edward Marsh*, p. 631.

4

THE PRINCIPLES OF GEORGIAN POETRY

If the early Georgians are, therefore, most easily defined through reference to what they opposed and if due allowance is made for their obvious unwillingness to be regarded as a "school," there is nevertheless a demonstrable sense in which they did in fact comprise a school.[1] There were fundamental poetic principles that they affirmed collectively, and these principles rested preeminently upon the intellectual convictions that Marsh and Brooke had formed at Cambridge.

The necessity of realism was the guiding conviction underlying the Georgian poetic. Since "realism" entails many meanings, however, and since the term has been variously applied to the Georgians, the brand of realism which they practiced must be fixed more precisely than historians of Georgian poetry have thus far managed. Most references to the realism of the Georgians have been misleading through their incompleteness. It is surely true that the Georgians employed a comparatively realistic vocabulary; and it is equally true that poets like Masefield, Gibson, and Brooke sought verisimilitude in their life studies. But the Georgians were governed as well by a more intellectually strenuous conception of

1. It is, of course, true that Edward Marsh denied the "smallest intention of founding a school, or of tracing a course for Poetry to follow" (*A Number of People* [New York, 1939], p. 322). But that denial must be interpreted in the light of Marsh's enterprise, which was to break through the "official" poetry then in favor. In urging poetic independence and the evaluation of poems on their own merits, he could hardly feel that founding a new movement was his intention. If, as Robert H. Ross scrupulously reminds us (*The Georgian Revolt, 1910-1922* [Carbondale, Ill., 1965], p. 237), the early Georgians did not comprise a "formal school," it may be argued that a poetic does not have to be wholly explicit. Especially among a small group of practicing poets and their empathic patron, it may exist as an understanding, an unstated harmony, no less real because uncodified. According to Christopher Hassall, "On hearing that Bottomley had been encouraging Rosenberg... Marsh intervened to make quite sure the senior Georgian was taking the right line with the boy" (*A Biography of Edward Marsh* [New York, 1959], p. 401).

realism, and even Ross's monumental account of the Georgians falls short of full clarification on this point.

In his preliminary characterization of Marsh's Georgians, Ross states that their "first concern was for truth to life, the quality which, for want of a more precise term, one is compelled to call realism." Realism, he says, was their "informing spirit"; it was "the quality most apparent in the verse of Masefield or Gibson, Abercrombie, Bottomley or Brooke."[2] At the point in his exposition where he attends most carefully to the distinguishing features of Marsh's early Georgian group, Ross observes that "above all, Georgianism in 1912-15 was synonymous with realism":

> Poetic realism, or truth to life, was the one feature which distinguished *Georgian Poetry* I and II from other contemporary anthologies and which gave the Georgians their most nearly unique hallmark. As it was exemplified in *Georgian Poetry* I and II, realism connoted two qualities, the first a state of mind in the poets themselves, the second a technique of writing verse. As a state of mind among the Georgian poets, realism came to mean primarily anti-sentimentalism. As a technique of verse writing it came to mean the inclusion in poetry of details, however nasty, which presumably possessed truth to reality as it was perceived by the five senses.[3]

So conceived, realism is a term in art criticism which legitimates the inclusion of ugliness into works of art. It declares a determination to broaden the range of art beyond the representation of beauty. It expresses an artistic intention to deal with the unattractive parts of life in a frank and honest manner. When commentators on the Georgian poets have noted their realism at all, it is to this dimension of the term that they have customarily made reference. Thus, we have many references to Brooke's description of seasickness in "A Channel Passage" ("Retchings twist and tie me,/Old meat, good meals, brown gobbets, up I throw") and of epic lovers grown old in "Menelaus and Helen" ("Her dry shanks twitch at Paris' mumbled name").[4] Thus, Georgian realism is

2. Ross, *The Georgian Revolt*, p. 24.
3. *Ibid.*, p. 125. See also p. 260, n. 27.
4. Geoffrey Keynes, ed., *The Poetical Works of Rupert Brooke* (London, 1946), pp. 113, 126. In his study of Flecker, Douglas Goldring observed, "The artist of to-day . . . is dissatisfied with much that might have given him pleasure a decade ago. He seeks more than what is at times contemptuously termed 'Beautiful Beauty'; and if he is taunted with accepting ugliness in its place, he can reply that what he seeks is significance – not the pretty Chinese lantern, but the naked light within" (*James Elroy Flecker* [London, 1922], p. 5).

exemplified by reference to Wilfrid Gibson's grim poetic studies of modern industrial life in *Daily Bread* (1910) and *Livelihood* (1917). Thus, Ralph Hodgson's "The Bull" is cited as an instance of the Georgians' unwillingness to ignore ugly details, of their ability to turn unpleasant particulars into poetry without sentimentalizing them. Thus, Masefield has been frequently identified as the chief exemplar of Georgian realism by reference to his highly influential depiction of so unlovely a character as Saul Kane in "The Everlasting Mercy" (1911). Grierson and Smith remark of the Masefield who wrote "The Everlasting Mercy," "No old far-off themes and stately diction for him, but common contemporary life in the raw, described in outspoken, almost brutal language."[5] And with approximately the same sense of the poem's realism, Ross has described "The Everlasting Mercy" as "the seminal work of the new realistic school."[6] But this conception of Georgian realism is too limited, too belletristic; it disregards the philosophic sense that also, and more significantly, informed the Georgians' view of realism.[7]

The brand of realism advocated by Marsh and Brooke was resonant with the philosophical accent of Moore and Russell. That is, the Georgians acknowledged a real world, external to them, the existence of which was not contingent upon their perception of it. But that world was available for their inspection, and the first principle of their realism was that they must attend carefully to the concrete particulars of external experience. Correlatively, they must learn to discipline the perceiving mind's tendency to immoderate generalization and abstraction. Marsh habitually expressed

5. Herbert J. C. Grierson and J. C. Smith, *A Critical History of English Poetry* (London, 1956), p. 491. In his account of Charles Sorley, one of the first of the realistic "trench poets," Middleton Murry makes this reference to Masefield's effect upon young poets in the years just preceding the first World War: "Sorley first appears before us radiant with the white-heat of a schoolboy enthusiasm for Masefield. Masefield is — how we remember the feeling! — the poet who has lived; his naked reality tears through 'the lace of putrid sentimentalism . . . which rotters like Tennyson and Swinburne have taught his (the superficial man's) soul to love.'" See J. Middleton Murry, *Aspects of Literature* (London, 1920), p. 160.

6. Ross, *The Georgian Revolt*, p. 13. See also p. 32. This simple view of Georgian realism as the unsentimental representation of contemporary life in the raw is also expressed by Hassall in his *Biography of Edward Marsh*, p. 684.

7. Ross approaches the sense in which Georgian realism possessed a philosophical dimension, an anti-idealist posture; but he blurs the point by relating it to anti-humanism and anti-romanticism without sufficient specificity. See *The Georgian Revolt*, pp. 16-17.

this anti-idealist bias in his editorial judgments. In a letter to Brooke, he offered this justification of a critical comment:

> By the way when I made my impertinent remark about your running Love to death ... I didn't mean love as a subject, but Love with a capital L as an abstraction, it seemed to be becoming a mannerism of style. [8]

The Georgian poet was advised to keep his eye upon the object itself, to maintain direct contact with experience. Marsh addressed even venerable Georgians, like de la Mare, in the same epistemological spirit:

> May I print, in *The Tryst*, "twixt the sleep and wake of Helen's dream" instead of "a Helen's dream?" To me, the sound is better, but that isn't the reason. In the rest of the poem all the people are mentioned as persons, not as types — Noah, Elijah, Leviathan — not a Noah, an Elijah, etc. — and this makes it so much more vivid — a real Paradise, not a Platonic or Hegelian abstraction. [9]

De la Mare eagerly conceded Marsh's point, and then reflected on his use of the indefinite article, "It's horrible after a moment's thought." [10] Brooke, writing to his friend Keeling in 1910, described his view of life thus:

> It consists in just looking at people and things as themselves — neither as useful nor moral nor ugly nor anything else, but just as being. At least that's a philosophical description of it. What happens is that I suddenly feel the extraordinary value and importance of everybody I meet, and almost everything I see. In *things* I am moved in this way especially by some things; but in people by almost all people. That is, when the mood is on me. I roam about places — yesterday I did it even in Birmingham! — and sit in trains and see the essential glory and beauty of all the

8. Quoted in Hassall, *A Biography of Edward Marsh*, p. 277. Brooke's own inhospitability to abstraction is wryly stated in "Tiare Tahiti," his mocking portrait of a paradise in which concrete particulars have disappeared into capitalized ideas or types: songs into Song, tears into Grief, lovers into Love, and feet into Ambulation. See Keynes, ed., *The Poetical Works of Rupert Brooke*, pp. 25-27.

9. *Ibid.*, pp. 471-472.

10. *Ibid.*, p. 472. Abercrombie revealed his consciousness of Marsh's philosophical stance when he wrote, "I hope you will like what I am doing: it is not very metaphysical." Letter from Lascelles Abercrombie to Edward Marsh, dated April 7 [1916?], in the Berg Collection of the New York Public Library.

people I meet. I can watch a dirty middle-aged tradesman in a
railway-carriage for hours, and love every dirty greasy sulky
wrinkle in his weak chin and every button on his spotted unclean
waistcoat. I know their states of mind are bad. But I'm so much
occupied with their being there at all, that I don't have time to
think of that. I tell you that a Birmingham goaty tariff-reform
fifth-rate business-man is splendid and desirable. It's the same
about the things of ordinary life. Half an hour's roaming about a
street or village or railway station shows so much beauty that it is
impossible to be anything but wild with suppressed exhilaration.
And it's not only beauty, and beautiful things. In a flicker of
sunlight on a blank wall, or a reach of muddy pavement, or
smoke from an engine at night there's a sudden significance and
importance and inspiration that makes the breath stop with a
gulp of certainty and happiness. It's not that the wall or the
smoke seem important for anything, or suddenly reveal any
general statement, or are rationally seen to be good and beautiful
in themselves — only that *for you* they're perfect and unique. It's
like being in love with a person. One doesn't (now-a-days, and if
one's clean-minded) think the person better or more beautiful or
larger than the truth. Only one is extraordinarily excited that the
person, exactly as he is, uniquely and splendidly just exists. It is a
feeling, not a belief. Only it is a feeling that has amazing results. I
suppose my occupation is being in love with the Universe — or
(for it is an important difference) with certain spots and moments
of it.[11]

Brooke's often quoted statement to Marsh (who never regarded

11. Geoffrey Keynes, ed., *The Letters of Rupert Brooke* (London, 1968),
pp. 258-259. De la Mare noted that nothing in Brooke's poetry "is more conspicuous
than its preoccupation with actual experience": "He is impatient of a vague idealism, as
wary as a fox of the faintest sniff of sentimentality. To avoid them . . . he flies to the
opposite extreme, and to escape from what he calls the rosy mists of poets' experience
emphasises the unpleasant side of life. His one desire is to tell each salient moment's
truth about it. Truth at all costs: let beauty take care of itself." "It is the moments," de
la Mare concludes, "that flower for Brooke. What is his poem 'Dining-room Tea' but the
lovely cage of an instant. . . . For truth's sake he has no fear of contradictions. The mood
changes, the problem, even the certainty shows itself under different aspects; he will be
faithful to each in turn." Walter de la Mare, *Rupert Brooke and the Intellectual
Imagination* (New York, 1920), pp. 15, 17-18. See also James Elroy Flecker's description of the true critic of poetry, in *Collected Prose* (London, 1920), pp. 246-247.
Although Abercrombie was not directly influenced by Cambridge realism, his philosophical dialogues provide another clear instance of the Georgian aversion to closed, narrowly
rationalistic systems of belief. They provide an equally clear example of his disposition
to regard knowing as intrinsically valuable and of his willingness to contemplate "Anything which in any man helps self-awareness to be joyously pleased with itself." Lascelles
Abercrombie, *Speculative Dialogues* (New York, 1913), p. 189. See especially the
dialogues entitled "Minos and a Ghost," "Science and the World," and "Philosophy and
the Angel."

sordidness as intrinsic with truth) in defense of his "unpleasant" poems is easily taken to be an expression of his commitment to artistic verisimilitude, that is, to the kind of simple representational realism that has been called the "hallmark" of Georgian poetry:

> There are common and sordid things — situations or details — that may suddenly bring all tragedy, or at least the brutality of actual emotions, to you. I rather grasp relievedly at them, after I've beaten vain hands in the rosy mists of poets' experiences.[12]

There is, as Hassall has concluded, a clear sense in which Brooke's realistic poems were attacks on Victorian social and literary decorum.[13] But they were something more: the intense and unmediated contemplation of reality. When the publisher Sidgwick objected to including "Libido" in Brooke's first volume, Brooke argued that to think the poem "improper" would constitute a misunderstanding of it:

> About a lot of the book I occasionally feel like Ophelia, that I've turned "Thought and affliction, passion, hell itself . . . to favour and to prettiness." So I'm extra keen about the places where I think that thought and passion are, however clumsily, *not* so transmuted. This was one of them. It seemed to have qualities of reality & novelty that made up for the clumsiness.[14]

As both these letters indicate, Brooke's emphasis was upon "actual emotions" rather than "sordid things." And Marsh, obviously concerned about possible misunderstanding of Brooke's remarks, felt it necessary — following his citation — to expand upon Brooke's explanation of his realism:

> To begin with, ugliness had a quite unaffected attraction for him; he thought it just as *interesting* as anything else; he didn't like it . . . but he liked thinking about it.[15]

Similarly, when reference is made to the realism of *King Lear's Wife*, one of the most controversial products of the early Georgian group, it is the drama's brutal action (Lear's death-room infidelity and Goneril's savage murder of Gormflaith) and coarse language

---

12. Edward Marsh, ed., *Rupert Brooke: The Collected Poems* (London, 1918), p. lxvi. Cf. Keynes, ed., *The Letters of Rupert Brooke*, pp. 327-329.
13. Christopher Hassall, *Rupert Brooke* (London, 1964), p. 539.
14. Keynes, ed., *The Letters of Rupert Brooke*, pp. 315-316.
15. Marsh, "Memoir," in *Rupert Brooke: The Collected Poems*, p. lxviii.

(the speech of the corpse-washers) that evidently alone justify the reference. Marsh assumed considerable editorial risk in his unhesitating decision to include it in the second volume of *Georgian Poetry*. He must have known that this drama would outrage even friends like Gosse and Squire. But the play so well illustrates Marsh's cognitive realism that it is not surprising that he continued to regard his publication of it as one of the genuine achievements of Georgian poetry.

What has not been noted in the inevitable comparisons of Gordon Bottomley's Lear with Shakespeare's is that the Georgian poet quite intentionally sacrificed the tragic majesty and breadth of Shakespeare's *interpretation* of human experience ("As flies to wanton boys, are we to the gods . . . ") to the accomplishment of a radically narrowed but more sharply particularized *statement* of human experience. As the play's title suggests, Bottomley's Lear is not the central character in an elaborately plotted action. Indeed, none of the main characters in *King Lear's Wife* is dominant. The dying Queen Hygd and her Artemis-like daughter Goneril combine with Lear to reveal through the circumstance of Lear's estrangement from his queen the motives peculiar to their respective ages, sexes, and conditions. Moreover, Bottomley's play does not strive "to produce the illusion of a thing happening as it would in real life," a task for which he thought prose fully adequate. Bottomley sought, rather, to show "that the nature of things can be depicted and attained on the stage without reconstructing the appearance of their actuality." "The poetic drama," he argued, "is, indeed, not so much a representation of a theme as a meditation upon it or a distillation from it; its business is far less the simulation of life than the evocation and isolation for our delight of the elements of beauty and spiritual illumination in the perhaps terrible and always serious theme chosen." He believed that the nature of things, "of poignantly real things happening to absorbingly real people," requires for its deepest portrayal chiefly the full exploitation of poetic language — including, for example, such "unnatural" devices as choral speech. For Bottomley, poetic language itself constituted the "action" of the play.[16]

Bottomley's conception of how reality was to be rendered disposed him to sacrifice cosmic typicality to the achievement of a

16. Gordon Bottomley, "Poetry and the Contemporary Theatre," *Essays and Studies by Members of the English Association*, 19 (Oxford, 1934), 139-140, 142-144.

more cross-grained character, who does not overshadow the other characters with his voluble rages and towering madness. It is difficult to generalize about Bottomley's Lear because the depiction dwells intensely upon moments of experience and states of mind, around which no ideological scaffolding has been constructed. This aspect of Georgian realism is, perhaps, partly responsible for the common charge that Georgian poetry lacked intellectual substance. What has been called triviality, however, was the early Georgian poet's characteristic reluctance to distort reality by inflating it with heroism or sentimentality or doctrine.

The principal feature of Georgian realism, therefore, is its very indifference to categories of experience (like the beautiful and the ugly) and to interpretations of experience (like the supernaturalist and the materialist). Made to seem reliable by the familiarity of accustomed usage, such schema were ignored by the Georgians as too remote from reality, as too facilely ordered to be entirely true. Confirmed pluralists who discounted the availability of any overarching transcendent truth, the early Georgians wished to engage reality item by item: to feel its shapes and textures, to perceive its distinctive forms, to grasp its essential meanings as fully and as directly as their sensibilities would allow. Thus, they sought to approximate the innocent eye of childhood, not as an artistic mannerism or as a means of escape from personal responsibility or from the modern world but as a model of the unaided sensibility.[17] For their conception of realism made them alert to the way in which conventional opinions normalize perception and obscure an unmediated view of reality. And, foremost, they wished to cultivate and to receive a naked vision of the world's continuing revelation. It is in this sense that de la Mare's "The Listeners"[18] is an outstanding example of Georgian realism

17. In an essay on Brooke, de la Mare offered this account of children as poets *manqués*: "Between their dream and their reality looms no impassable abyss. There is no solitude more secluded than a child's, no absorption more complete, no insight more exquisite and, one might even add, more comprehensive. As we strive to look back and to live our past again, can we recall any joy, fear, hope or disappointment so extreme as those of our childhood, any love more impulsive and unquestioning, and, alas, any boredom so unmitigated and unutterable?" (*Rupert Brooke and the Intellectual Imagination*, p. 8).

18. [Edward Marsh, ed.], *Georgian Poetry: 1911-1912* (London, 1912), pp. 71-72. The poem "affirmed the reality of the undefined," according to Sidney Cox in his report of Robert Frost's great admiration of "The Listeners." See Sidney Cox, *A Swinger of Birches* (New York, 1957), p. 6. Cf. Harold Monro's discussion of de la Mare in *Some Contemporary Poets* (London, 1920), pp. 61-64.

despite its manifest distance from the "unpleasant" poems of Masefield, Bottomley, Gibson, and Brooke. It is in this sense that Georgian realists found the world both joyous and doleful, dealt with both primroses and urban grayness, celebrated both hard fact and airy fantasy. Thus, the W. H. Davies who wrote with such unaffected sweetness of the pastoral landscape in "Days Too Short" and "In May" could also evoke the uttermost despair of a London beggar in "The Heap of Rags."[19] It is this sense of Georgian realism as a particular angle of vision, as the refinement of *how* rather than *what* the poet sees,[20] that will enable us to understand D. H. Lawrence's membership in the early Marsh group and that will help us better to understand what it was that drew poets like Edward Thomas and Robert Frost to the Georgians. Although Lawrence dissented from Marsh's heavy insistences upon the necessity of form in art, he shared Marsh's view of the relation of art to reality:

> The essence of poetry with us in this age of stark and unlovely actualities is a stark directness, without a shadow of a lie, or a shadow of deflection anywhere. Everything can go, but this stark, bare, rocky directness of statement, this alone makes poetry, today.[21]

It must be added that the philosophical sense in which the Georgians practiced realism made them indifferent not only to categorical and interpretive abstractions from experience. They were also ahistorical, indifferent to the more transient and parochial forms of experience, since these — like conventional beliefs — were only the outer garments of reality or ephemeral distortions of it. As Bottomley put it, "My business has seemed to be to look

---

19. [Marsh, ed.], *Georgian Poetry: 1911-1912*, pp. 60-62. Although Davies — like others of the Georgian company — is generally regarded as an innocuous triller of simple nature lyrics, he has written poems like "The Dark Hour," "The Idiot and the Child," and "Love's Rivals," which in their aching gloom and irony of circumstance are remarkably close to the poetry of Hardy. See *The Complete Poems of W. H. Davies* (London, 1963), pp. 98, 100, 466.

20. As my account of the reputation of Georgian poetry indicates, this philosophical dimension of Georgian realism is still largely unrecognized by historians and critics of contemporary poetry. Indeed, they have been too seldom aware of the more obvious sense in which the Georgians were realists.

21. Letter to Catherine Carswell, dated January 11, 1916, in Harry T. Moore, ed., *The Collected Letters of D. H. Lawrence* (New York, 1962), I, 413.

for the essentials of life, the part that does not change."[22] So conceived, realism demands more than the mere recording of experience. It proceeds, rather, beyond faithful reports to the discrimination of essential details, beyond the data that constitute the material or psychic factuality of experience to those elemental truths ineluctably resident in events and perceptions. Hence, we have the Georgians' interest in nature, in the rhythm of the seasons, in love and birth and death, in the enigmas of personality, in the dependably certain and the dependably uncertain:

> O, years and tides and leagues and all their billows
> Can alter not man's knowledge of men's hearts —
> While trees and rocks and clouds include our being
> We know the epics of Atlantis still:
> A hero gave himself to lesser men,
> Who first misunderstood and murdered him,
> And then misunderstood and worshipped him;
> A woman was lovely and men fought for her,
> Towns burnt for her, and men put men in bondage,
> But she put lengthier bondage on them all;
> A wanderer toiled among all the isles
> That fleck this turning star of shifting sea,
> Or lonely purgatories of the mind,
> In longing for his home or his lost love.[23]

The frequently remarked fondness of the Georgians for pastoral settings was, consequently, a function of their brand of realism, not an expression of their flight from reality. In natural surroundings they felt themselves less distracted by contemporary and historical fashions, and thus better able to grasp and penetrate those endlessly recurring experiences most central and urgent to our humanity. To put it differently, while the Georgian realist was inhospitable to the abstract generalization and the monistic synthesis, he was also wary of the flatness and triviality into which

---

22. Gordon Bottomley, *Poems and Plays* (London, 1953), p. 12. See also Bottomley's letter to William Rothenstein, in *Since Fifty: Recollections of William Rothenstein* (London, 1939), III, 124-128.

23. Gordon Bottomley, *Poems of Thirty Years* (London, 1925), p. 1.

the mere iteration of particularized detail might lead him. His "centrist" brand of realism impelled him toward the recognition and definition of "unmatched moments":

> I have understood that I desire from art
> And from creation not repeated things
> Of every day, not the mean content
> Or discontent of average helpless souls,
> Not passionate abstractions of loveliness,
> But unmatched moments and exceptional deeds
> And all that cannot happen every day.[24]

No less than the simpler representational realism of the "unpleasant" poems, this subtler philosophical realism was shared by Marsh and Brooke; and it served as a kind of touchstone in the formation of the original Georgian group.[25]   For example, in explanation of his choice of a lyric for inclusion in *Georgian Poetry*, Marsh wrote:

> *Nearness* for instance impresses me most deeply as a formally perfect and emotionally poignant rendering of the universal human consciousness that the individual is alone, even when in the most utter communion with someone else.[26]

Properly understood, then, realism is the first principle of the Georgian poetic; and the three remaining principles are all best comprehended in relation to this governing conviction.

Within the Georgian poetic, poetry — and, indeed, art in gen-

---

24. *Ibid.*, p. 129.

25. Contrary to their reputation as idealess warblers, the Georgians — Cantabrigian or not — were drawn to philosophic discussion. For example, Maurice Browne recalled an occasion at Marsh's rooms in June of 1914 when Brooke, Abercrombie, Monro, and Gibson "talked metaphysics . . . the night through." He adds that "Brooke's grasp and handling of intellectual abstractions was much more than unusual, but he was a child in the philosophical hands of Abercrombie, perhaps the most compelling, conversationally, of contemporary British metaphysicians." Maurice Browne, *Recollections of Rupert Brooke* (Chicago, 1927), p. 40.

26. Letter from Marsh to John Freeman, quoted in Hassall, *A Biography of Edward Marsh*, p. 464. Such a conception of realism was not, of course, easily apprehended by those who naively supposed the realist in literature to address himself in an indecorous, colloquial style to the sordid and painful features of contemporary society. Thus, ironically enough, the epithet "escapist" has been commonly applied to members of the early Marsh group — like Brooke and Bottomley — whose commitment to realism was fundamental. For a good discussion, in this connection, of Bottomley's realism, see R. A. Scott-James, *Fifty Years of English Literature: 1900-1950*, 2d ed. (London, 1956), pp. 113-114.

eral — was held to possess a unique function, a claim that rested upon the recognition that science and poetry engage reality differently, that ethical directives and poetic admonitions are meant to produce different consequences. Like Moore and Russell, the Georgians recognized that art possesses intrinsic value as a means of embodying those areas of experience and states of mind less available to the senses than to the imagination, less immediately available to reason than to intuition. While the Georgians would doubtless have rejected as insufficiently tough-minded the Romantic idealism of Wordsworth and Emerson, they would have accepted the psychological validity of Emerson's assertion in *Nature* that experience is not adequately described through recourse alone to the principles of carpentry and chemistry. They acknowledged, in other words, the existence of events in human experience that are not amenable to — that defy — literal statement and objective verification, that can only be approached analogically and fictively. They, accordingly, regarded true poetry as functionally distinct from other forms of cognition and statement. They regarded the vocation of poetry sui generis, as the dedicated endeavor to dilate and clarify those real events in human consciousness that could not have been as adequately expressed in non-poetic form. Thus, the Georgians differentiated poetic statements from scientific statements: as human beings, the scientist and the poet confront the same world; but as scientists and poets, they attend to different parts of that world, employ different kinds of vision and language. Thus, the Georgians also differentiated poetic statements from ethical statements in terms of their separate intentions and bases of value. They understood the poetic statement as intended only to provide a truthful and resonant embodiment of experience, and they understood the ethical statement as intended to serve as a *means* of directing human behavior. Consequently, they held the poetic statement's worth to be intrinsic, self-contained, establishable without reference to anything outside of it; while the ethical statement's worth was held to be established pragmatically, in terms of its effect or consequences.

This second principle of the Georgian poetic is articulated most explicitly in the critical writings of Lascelles Abercrombie. The only member of the early Georgian group who provided a systematic elaboration of his artistic beliefs,[27] Abercrombie begins by positing a level of human experience that he calls aesthetic experience. Art, he says, originates always in "an actual and casual experience of a certain kind: actual in the psychological sense, which of course includes imaginary events; and casual in the sense that it is something inexplicably given to us, part of the uncalculated fact of living."[28] Aesthetic experience is a "universal aspect of all mental action."[29] It is not properly restricted to the sense of beauty, but is to be conceived much more broadly.[30] Aesthetic experience, then, is experience at what is virtually the threshold of consciousness, that primary stage of perception at which the human response to experience is most direct and unaffected. It is experience in its most immediate terms, prior to rationalization and moralization where it is not actually insusceptible to such translations:

> it is experience simply as such, valued for its own sake without reference to any judgment as to its truth or reality or moral goodness. And anything at all can be an aesthetic experience: even matter which is on its way to intellectual or moral judgment can be that, so long as it is taken at its face-value, simply as pure experience — simply as something which is just happening in one's mind. It is the primary fact of conscious life that we are first of all interested in things happening simply because they do happen: this is the interest of experience in its aesthetic aspect, and it requires no justification except itself.[31]

The human judgment can make rational, ethical, and aesthetic determinations of experience. Because these determinations are

27. "I am doing a complete Poetics for my lectures. When they are done there will be no need for no one to argue no more. All will be settled." Letter from Lascelles Abercrombie to Edward Marsh, dated August 27, 1919, in the Berg Collection of the New York Public Library.

28. Lascelles Abercrombie, *An Essay towards a Theory of Art* (London, 1922), p. 13.

29. *Ibid.*, p. 14.

30. *Ibid.*, pp. 14-15, 26, 30, 33, 35-36, 59-60. This comprehensive conception of beauty enabled the early Georgians to attend to the "unpleasant" features of experience without their feeling constrained to dichotomize prettiness and "truth." That is, "aesthetic experience" was taken to be experience of the object in and for itself, be it a rose or a garbage can.

31. *Ibid.*, p. 30.

made by the same faculty, unfortunately they are sometimes confused.[32] Art, however, is appropriately only concerned with "the expression of aesthetic experience."[33] It is that expression of experience which serves no ulterior purpose, which does not "look outside itself for its value":[34]

> Expression for its own sake, then, — expression that carries its own justification — that does not need to go beyond itself in order to *make good*: that seems to be the condition under which a work of art can occur.[35]

Art exists to gratify the desire of human beings to state their immediate experience significantly.[36] Its function is to extend consciousness and understanding at the level of experience itself. Thus, Abercrombie observes that "the poet's business is not to describe things to us, or tell us about things; but to create in our minds the very things themselves."[37] And de la Mare says, "All lyrical poetry beats with the heart, tells not of things coldly and calmly considered, but of things seen and felt in a sudden clearness of the senses."[38]

It was the definition and the illumination of this realm of being that the Georgians took to be the unique function of poetry. Unlike such experimental Modernists as the Edith Sitwell of *Wheels*, the Georgians did not argue the necessary separation of modern poetry from traditional poetry by appealing to the unprecedented character of contemporary life. Rather, the Georgians argued the necessary separation of nonpoetic from poetic statements by appealing to the structure of human experience.

Having asserted art's general concern with the expression of aesthetic experience, Abercrombie specifies poetry as the only art

32. *Ibid.*, p. 34.
33. *Ibid.*, p. 44.
34. *Ibid.*, p. 22.
35. *Ibid.*, p. 19.
36. For Abercrombie's definition of artistic significance, see *An Essay towards a Theory of Art*, pp. 103-104. See also Abercrombie's *The Theory of Poetry* (London, 1924), pp. 202-210. "For just as each item of the experience is valued immediately and intuitively, so the interrelatedness of the items is valued; and this latter inclusive value (inclusive, but equally immediate) is our sense of the significance of the experience — a sense of face-value significance which, just because it is immediate, is much more satisfying than any intellectual construction of significance" (p. 210).
37. Lascelles Abercrombie, *Poetry: Its Music and Meaning* (London, 1932), p. 47.
38. Quoted in Scott-James, *Fifty Years of English Literature*, p. 117.

"whereby experience can be transferred whole and unimpaired, in all its subtlety and complexity, from one mind to another." [39] "The whole purpose of a poet's technique," he adds, "is to make a moment of his experience come to life in other minds than his." [40]

> When therefore we come across language which is instinct with an exceptional degree of meaning; when it not only conveys ideas or the way things happened, but can make those ideas enact themselves in our imagination as sensuous and emotional experiences, or can turn the way things happened into the very sense of their happening: when language does this, we recognize that we have poetry before us.[41]

> The art of poetry endeavours to make language not so much the vehicle of thought as the equivalent of experience itself; and it can only do so by deliberately using every quality which language is capable of exhibiting — and by using, as far as possible, all the qualities appropriate to its purpose simultaneously.[42]

Because aesthetic experience is uncategorized, plural, a blend of mystery and fact, it is — of the several determinations of experience — the hardest to conceptualize precisely and to communicate accurately. But it is just this that is the unique function of the artist; and it is the poet whose medium — the richly particularized instrument of language — would seem to afford a marked advantage. Therefore, the Georgian discipline required of the poet unremitting dedication to his craft.

The Georgians perceived two notable misuses of poetry which obscured and distorted its distinctive purpose. First, they regarded as mistaken the view that poetry is a vehicle of intellectual analysis or instruction or exhortation; and they, accordingly, rejected the conception of the poet as philosopher or teacher or prophet. They regarded as mistaken the conventional belief that poetry is an attractive and persuasive means of communicating philosophical, moral, and civil doctrines; for they recognized that this belief made of the poet a kind of rhetorician and reduced poetry to a largely ornamental function. Thus, they were acutely aware that

39. Abercrombie, *The Theory of Poetry*, p. 16.
40. *Ibid.*, p. 102.
41. *Ibid.*, pp. 116-117.
42. *Ibid.*, p. 148.

the appearance of poetic form and technique was no guarantee of the presence of poetry.[43] It was from this perspective that the Georgians found many traditionally approved poets — like the Victorian public bards — to be something less than "true" poets. Such poets seemed to the Georgians to have served ethics or patriotism or theology to the virtual exclusion of what Abercrombie called aesthetic experience. Consequently, their poems were poetry only in the formal sense; and when their use of poetic language was not merely ornamental it was something worse, the rhetorician's snares. Partly in reaction to the aestheticism of the Pre-Raphaelites and the Decadents, such eminently popular late Victorian conservatives as Kipling, Henry Newbolt, Watson, and Alfred Austin stressed — together with their large, admiring public — the necessity of distinguishing between form and content, between the message and its vehicle. This distinction, widely practiced and widely accepted, made it possible to value poems chiefly by reference to the "soundness" of their doctrines.[44] Committed, however, to a poetic that postulated a distinctive function and an intrinsic value for poetry, the Georgians collectively opposed this fundamental distortion. In 1910, when Galsworthy's *Justice* was stimulating support for prison reform, Marsh and Galsworthy met at a dinner party. The question of didactic art having arisen on that occasion, Marsh put to Galsworthy a central Georgian question: would he prefer to write a play that would transform the prison system and be forgotten or one that had no practical effect but would survive as a work of art.[45] In 1913, Flecker made this typically Georgian judgment upon versified morality:

> This importunity of the "message" . . . has corrupted nearly all our artists, from William Wordsworth down to the latest writers of manly tales in verse. If we have preaching to do, in heaven's name let us call it a sermon and write it in prose.[46]

Abercrombie makes the same point more temperately:

43. *Ibid.*, pp. 26-27.
44. See C. K. Stead, *The New Poetic* (London, 1964), pp. 71, 77-78. For a Georgian critique of this divorce, see Abercrombie, *The Theory of Poetry*, pp. 47-49.
45. Hassall, *A Biography of Edward Marsh*, p. 167.
46. Flecker, *Collected Prose*, p. 240.

> Poetry may, among a thousand other things, do some occasional teaching: but if it does, it is not by virtue of its instruction that it is poetry, and the instruction would probably fare better elsewhere.[47]

Alternatively, the Georgians regarded the distinctive function of poetry as obscured or distorted by poets who mistakenly understood the pronouncement of the didactic heresy to justify either a highly subjective poetry or a pure, contentless poetry. The Georgians have often been likened to the Pre-Raphaelites and the Decadents by critics who have observed their common antididacticism, their mutual desire to liberate poetry from the uses of public morality. Indeed, the frequent charge of escapism — of indifference to the great issues of their own time — that has been lodged against the Georgians derives importantly from this linkage. It should be noted, however, that whenever the Georgians characteristically made favorable reference to what may be broadly termed the "aesthetic" movement in English poetry, it was usually in relation to the general reluctance of poets like Rossetti or Dowson or Swinburne to subordinate art to some other kind of truth. But the obsessiveness and vacuity of much aesthetic poetry struck the Georgians as yet another way of violating art's proper relation to experience, as a deflection from the reality that the true poet endeavors to confront. In their veneration of archaic attitudes and language, their self-conscious artistic posturing, their limited conception of beauty, their preoccupation with sensuality, the aesthetes seemed to the Georgians to have turned their angle of vision inward, to have taken their eyes off the object. The resulting poetry was too private, too emotional[48] when it was not meaningless. In 1913, Marsh offered Siegfried Sassoon the following criticism of his verses:

> I think it certain that you have a lovely instrument to play upon and no end of beautiful tunes in your head, but that sometimes you write them down without getting enough meaning into them to satisfy the mind. Sometimes the poems are like pearls, with enough grit in the middle to make the nucleus of a durable work, but too often they are merely beautiful soap-bubbles which burst as soon as one has had time to admire the colors.[49]

47. Abercrombie, *The Theory of Poetry*, p. 45.
48. Flecker, *Collected Prose*, p. 239.
49. Quoted in Siegfried Sassoon, *The Weald of Youth* (New York, 1942), pp. 129-130.

In this same letter, Marsh describes the poetry of Rossetti, Swinburne, and Dowson as of the "vague iridescent ethereal kind." He promptly adds, "It seems a necessity now to write either with one's eye on an object or with one's mind at grips with a more or less definite idea."[50] Abercrombie, after disavowing didactic poetry, is equally intent upon urging the unacceptability of matterless poetry. "The art of poetry," he says, "consists both of having something to say and of saying it."[51] Referring to Swinburne as "the type of poet who exhibits art without matter," Abercrombie states that "Art without matter can only be, in poetry, language without meaning."[52]

Thus, the Georgians' belief that poetry serves a unique function in attending to a specific realm or level of human experience, which art appropriately expresses, led them to narrow the scope of poetry by requiring its true practitioners to restrict themselves, as artists, to that function. In this sense, their poetry was literally radical. Their often remarked narrowness was a matter of poetic principle, relatable to their desire to dissociate poetry from abstraction and rhetoric, on the one hand, from meaninglessness and personal expression, on the other.[53] They restricted their poetry to the concrete, to what they had experienced, to what they perceived as objectively existent and humanly relevant, to what intrinsically compelled expression and communication. True poetry, according to the Georgians, was not produced by poets ambitious to gratify the public or egocentrically impelled toward private catharsis or merely proficient in the mechanics of verse-making. When Marsh cited "intensity of 'thought or feeling'"[54] as one of the criteria governing his editorial decisions, he implied that the true poet composes because he must, because he experiences something with such peculiar urgency and such undeniable relevance to the human condition that it demands communication.

In relation, then, to the distinctive function of poetry and out of a keen awareness of the two principal ways in which poetry had

50. *Ibid.*, p. 130.
51. Abercrombie, *The Theory of Poetry*, p. 113.
52. *Ibid.*, p. 116. Abercrombie also attacks the notion of art as personal expression. True art, he says, is an act of communication; and what is entirely personal in its significance cannot be communicated. See Abercrombie, *An Essay towards a Theory of Art*, pp. 45-49.
53. See Stead, *The New Poetic*, pp. 29, 82-87, although Stead does not emphasize sufficiently the dissociation from the aesthetes.
54. Marsh, *A Number of People*, p. 323.

been commonly betrayed into serving other causes, the Georgians attempted to define and to cultivate the mental set most conducive to the composition of true poetry. It was in this connection — and not out of mindless traditionalism — that they spoke of the state of inspiration or trance as a desideratum of the poetic process. As rationalists and agnostics, the Georgians did not of course think of the poet as inspired in either the Platonic or the Christian sense. Rather, their idea of a poetic trance is simply the recognition that the poet composes in an unusual state of mind, in which he perceives more than he normally would, in which his sensibility is exceptionally heightened and his ability to integrate the particulars of experience receives a fresh access of authority. At such moments, the poet is, metaphorically speaking, in a state of inspiration. This notion was essential to the Georgians' insistence that it is the poet's function to engage experience clearly and objectively; for it is precisely when the mind is fully absorbed in the immediate contemplation of reality that it serves neither doctrine nor self. In just such moments, subjective consciousness comes closest to extinction or is transformed briefly into a more comprehensive sentience.[55] What Spender has remarked of de la Mare applies as well to much early Georgian poetry: it possesses an intensely dreamlike quality, akin to a state of trance, through which experience has been rendered impersonally and objectively.[56] Abercrombie assigns primary importance to inspiration in poetic composition, noting that "every poem, big or little, if it is to have the slightest value for us, must have been, as we say, *inspired.*"[57]

The third principle of the Georgian poetic is a corollary of the Georgians' conception of realism and poetic function, for they conceived of the true poet as an independent whose single allegiance is to the achievement of poetic truth. As A. C. Benson pointed out in 1913, they wrote "without deference or sub-

---

55. As I have noted in chapter 3, above, this conception of art as disinterested contemplation was also central to Imagist poetics. See T. E. Hulme, "Bergson's Theory of Art," in *Speculations*, ed. Herbert Read (London, 1924).

56. Stephen Spender, *The Struggle of the Modern* (London, 1963), pp. 162-163.

57. Abercrombie, *The Theory of Poetry*, p. 27. The nature and role of inspiration in poetry are discussed at length by Abercrombie in this book. See Chapter I, pp. 27-40; and Chapter II, pp. 41-76.

servience."[58]   Under the direct or indirect influence of Moore and
Russell, they regarded independence as a requisite virtue since it
disposed them to examine themselves and the surrounding world
freely and honestly, without the intermediate distortions of self or
public commitment. The early Marsh group's assertion of poetic
independence became a kind of collective measure of their artistic
integrity and courage because it required them, as poets, to cultivate a detachment that earned them the suspicion and hostility of
traditionalists and Modernists alike.

The Georgian poet did not indulge the public's conventionalized
appetites, as Watson and Noyes were doing, by repeating familiar
poetic formulas: he was not to be directed in the act of expression
by consideration of the public's response to his work.[59]   That is,
while poetry is indisputably an act of communication, the value of
the communication depends crucially upon the independence of
its originator. Consequently, even in his socialist argument for
government support of artists, Brooke repudiated the conception
of the artist as a public agent:

> There is another wrong notion of art that falsifies the opinions of
> many on this subject. Let us beware of those who talk of "the art
> of the people," or of "expressing the soul of the Community."
> The Community hasn't got a soul; you can't voice the soul of the
> Community any more than you can blow its nose. The conditions
> of Democracy may profoundly alter the outlook of many artists,
> and partly their style and subject matter. But the *main* business
> of art has been, is, and, one must assume, will be an individual
> and unique affair. "I saw — *I* saw," the artist says, "a tree against
> the sky, or a blank wall in the sunlight, and it was so thrilling, so
> arresting, so particularly itself, that —well really, I *must* show
> you! ... There!" Or the writer explains, "Just so and just so it
> happened, or might happen, and thus the heart shook, and
> thus ..." And suddenly, deliciously, with them you see and
> feel.[60]

The Georgian neither wooed nor rejected the public audience for

---

58. Quoted in Hassall, *A Biography of Edward Marsh*, p. 682.
59. See Abercrombie, *An Essay towards a Theory of Art*, pp. 64-65.
60. Rupert Brooke, *Democracy and the Arts* (London, 1946), pp. 6-7. Paper read to
the Cambridge University Fabian Society in 1910.

poetry; he attempted, rather, to indicate the proper relationship between the poet and his audience.

Moreover, the Georgian poet did not indulge immoderately his own sensorium, his fascination with private details of experience, as Marinetti and some of the Imagists had done: he was not to be misled into the madness of subjectivism. Since they acknowledged poetry to be a form of communication, the Georgians attempted also to indicate the proper relationship between the poet and his poem. That is, while poetry is clearly the expression of experience, the value of the expression depends critically upon the objective reality of the experience. As an artist, the true poet serves only the truth that is distinctively apprehended by art.

Thus, when the Georgians avowed the poet's primary dedication to his craft, his independence of literary schools and the public, they were not simply restating the position of the "aesthetes." Rather, they were asserting the principle that independence is essential to the poet's vision and expression of experience; and that, consequently, there is no prior or more exalted claim upon his fidelity than that of his muse. Speaking of the contributors to *Georgian Poetry*, Peter Quennell says that "each was primarily a writer of verse, pursuing his art with a wholehearted passion which the political passions of the 'thirties had not yet begun to dilute and cloud."[61]   And Harold Monro began his discussion of contemporary poetry in 1920 with an attack on those fashionable young poets dedicated only to the service of ambition and the achievement of acclaim.[62]

In contrast with poets who followed approved channels — whether old or new — and pursued the main chance, the detached quality of the early Georgians made them often appear willful, inconsistent, and odd. But from their independent position, they felt better able to contemplate reality, to see the actual features of aesthetic experience and to communicate them honestly. Despite his government office and personal view that the war was justified, Marsh helped Siegfried Sassoon both to publish his antiwar poems and to circumvent the difficulties arising from his protest.[63] Indeed, after reading the manuscript of Sassoon's *Counter-Attack,*

61. Peter Quennell, *The Sign of the Fish* (New York, 1960), p. 28.
62. Monro, *Some Contemporary Poets*, pp. 9-15.
63. See Siegfried Sassoon, *Siegfried's Journey: 1916-1920* (New York, 1946), pp. 42, 58, 115.

his most unrelievedly harsh collection of antiwar poems, Marsh
wrote to Sassoon expressing dissent from the advice of Sassoon's
publisher that the book's savagery be mitigated by the inclusion of
some pleasant poems:

> I think Heinemann is quite wrong in wanting the book stuffed up
> with things foreign to its present character. It's of its essence that
> it should produce its own effect, which it can only do by keeping
> homogeneous.[64]

As the letter indicates, Marsh was able and willing to distinguish
between the national interest and the interests of poetry, and he
did so habitually. Despite his opposition to what seemed to him
the anarchic experimentalism of the literary left wing, Marsh in
1916 successfully supported the securing of a treasury grant for
James Joyce.[65] Whether as patron or literary editor, Marsh was
entirely dedicated to poetry, consistently independent in his judgments. Despite the occasional outcry of his wounded sense of
propriety, he persisted in his conviction that poetry was to be
judged by fundamental poetic standards. Writing to one of his
fallen-away Georgians, Marsh provided this self-characterization:

> But one of the many differences between us is that my first love
> has always been and always will be what you stigmatize as
> literature and poetizing, whereas you care first and foremost for
> "idea."[66]

The independent spirit in which Marsh edited *Georgian Poetry*,
the extent to which the contributors to the early volumes were
chosen for their primary dedication to poetry, has gone almost
unremarked. Perhaps only Stead has thus far pointed in the right
direction:

> The fact that, at a time when patriotic feeling had become
> hysterical, Edward Marsh printed the best of Sassoon's poems
> despite their "unpatriotic" sentiment and their use of words like
> "syphilitic," is surely further evidence that justice has not been
> done to him as an anthologist.[67]

64. Quoted in Hassall, *A Biography of Edward Marsh*, p. 438.
65. *Ibid.*, pp. 400-401.
66. *Ibid.*, p. 507.
67. Stead, *The New Poetic*, p. 89.

Marsh's heart and mind went out, almost compulsively, to poets whose signal quality was their independent service to the muse. It is easy, therefore, to understand his quick recognition of the unappreciated merits of de la Mare, Davies, Bottomley, and Abercrombie; his ready acceptance of Brooke's friend Flecker. The literary behavior attributed to Flecker by a contemporary illustrates very well his claim, and theirs, upon Marsh's loyalty:

> He was, as far as I know, completely without ulterior motive or base ambitions. He never could have played the now too familiar game of literary and social intrigue by which verse-writers of only moderate talent inflate themselves into great figures. His conception of what is required of those who practise the art of poetry would have made any such proceeding simply unthinkable — a game for bagmen, not for kings.[68]

Like the other early Georgians, Flecker "was never fashionable, never joined any mutual admiration society, and never depended, for inspiration, upon the reactions of any gang or clique":

> As a poet he stood upon his own feet. He followed his own path, looking neither to the right nor to the left, and as soon as he had "found himself" he was apparently but little influenced by any of his contemporaries.[69]

The last principle of the Georgian poetic, exacting craftsmanship and concern for form, is — like the third principle — a corollary of the first two. But hostile critics have usually pronounced the Georgians' manifest attention to matters of form and technique the badge of their enervated traditionalism; while friendlier critics, with equal simplicity, have suggested that the Georgians' single virtue was their effort to up-date the language of poetry by purging it of archaism and an unnatural syntax. It was the Georgians' full conception of what realism entailed, however, their awareness of poetry's distinctive function, and their consequent sense of the necessary independence and dedication of the poet that made them particularly conscious of the heavy burden that their medium must bear. And it was this consciousness that drew their attention to the problem of form, to the mechanics of

68. Goldring, *James Elroy Flecker*, p. 67.
69. *Ibid.*, pp. 125, 126.

poetic expression. Collectively, the Georgians accepted painstaking care in lexical selection, syntactic placement, and metrical practice as the absolute obligation of any true poet, that is, of any poet dedicated to the honest communication of aesthetic experience.

Indeed, if poetic craftsmanship is the one aspect of Georgian poetry that all of its commentators have remarked, that may be because it is the most tangible principle of their poetic, and hence the one most easily framed in explicit terms. Thus, in a retrospective account of Marsh's literary principles, Robert Graves stressed Marsh's preoccupation with formal precision:

> Everything must mean what it says; the ear must never be cheated, or the reason offended; punctuation must be exact, diction clean, metaphors and quotations accurate.[70]

And in an admonitory letter to one of his younger Georgians who had commenced to stray, Marsh invoked Brooke as a proper model by noting "how Rupert used to go over everything, test every sentence for what could be left out and what could be put with more verve and force."[71] Goldring's specification of Flecker as "a superb craftsman with a real devotion to his art"[72] is essentially what every other critic has conceded to virtually every other member of Marsh's early circle.

Poetic craftsmanship was not, however, their end; it was, rather, the means of defining and communicating their unmediated perceptions of aesthetic experience with maximal resonance, objectivity, and clarity. Canby's observation that Frost's poems are "ways of seeing and saying the truth"[73] is equally applicable to

---

70. Christopher Hassall and Denis Mathews, comps., *Eddie Marsh: Sketches for a Composite Literary Portrait* (London, 1953), p. 25.

71. Quoted in Hassall, A *Biography of Edward Marsh,* p. 508. According to de la Mare, Brooke was a poet "who never spared mind and spirit in the effort to do the best work he could ... a true craftsman delighting in his job" (*Rupert Brooke and the Intellectual Imagination,* p. 22). On Brooke's dedication to poetic craftsmanship, see also Timothy Rogers, *Rupert Brooke: A Reappraisal and Selection* (London, 1971), pp. 180-183.

72. Goldring, *James Elroy Flecker,* p. 68. In his obituary of Flecker, Brooke noted that Flecker's poetry had gained in "clearness" as it progressed and that his craftsmanship had become "singularly accurate." See John Sherwood, *No Golden Journey: A Biography of James Elroy Flecker* (London, 1973), p. 222.

73. Henry Seidel Canby, *American Memoir* (Boston, 1947), p. 310. Frost was, in fact, proposed by Gibson to Marsh as a contributor to *Georgian Poetry.* Now that the

the early Georgians. That is, the Georgians discriminated between conception and technique, between the immediate apprehension of experiential significance and the act of verbal definition. Moreover, the act of verbal definition proceeded from the personal act of expression to the public act of communication; and the Georgians recognized that at either of these two stages what had been experienced independently and illuminatingly might be distorted or obscured through the inexpert employment of language. Abercrombie says that "each inspiration is something which did not, and could not, originally exist as words":

> Verbal thought has nothing to do with it. It is as experience — imaginative experience — that poetry begins. And by "imagination," I do not mean that it belongs necessarily to the unsubstantial daydreams of pure fantasy; I mean an experience which, long after its first occurrence, has been continued in the poet's mind by imagination — by the power, namely, of holding something constantly before the mind in keen and vivid definition. I mean also, when I call this experience imaginative, to imply very emphatically that it has not been prolonged as a train of reasoning or reflection, not as an intellectual topic, but simply as experience immediately enjoyable or exciting in itself. It is not the rational or practical or moral value of things that supplies the inspiration of poetry with its energy; but the primitive unquestioned instant value any experience has on the face of it, as a moment when *that which knows* delights to exert itself.[74]

Whatever has been thus accepted, brings with it a certain joy and

studies of Hassall, Ross, and Stead have prepared the way for a more accurate examination of the Georgians, the existing appraisals of the relationship between Frost and some of the early Georgians will undoubtedly bear revision and extension. By the same token, the belated discovery of Frost as a grimly realistic poet, only fictively pastoral, who explores the dreadful features of human experience, has already led one critic to reestablish the connection between Frost and the early Georgians. M. L. Rosenthal says that the staple of Frost's reputation is his "lyrical and realistic repossession of the rural and the 'natural.' . . . But beneath the surface appeal there lurks a further and terrifying implication. . . . The consciousness at work in his poetry is neither that of a plain New England farmer nor that of a Romantic rediscoverer of primitive delights. His is still the modern mind in search of its own meanings. The aim is comparable to that of the Georgians, among whom Frost first found kindred sensibilities and became certain of his true bearings." See M. L. Rosenthal, *The Modern Poets* (New York, 1960), pp. 110-111; and Glen A. Love, "Frost's 'The Census-Taker' and de la Mare's 'The Listeners,' " *Papers on Language and Literature*, 4 (Spring 1968), 198-200.

74. Abercrombie, *The Theory of Poetry*, pp. 62, 64.

excitement, to which is due the urgency it takes on in the poet's mind, driving him to express it in some appropriate form.[75]

And this is required not because form in poetry is conventional, or expected by a sort of etiquette; but because the form of a poem is its way of communicating to us something essential in the poet's inspiration. The form of a poem is a necessary contribution to its meaning, for it conveys the peculiar unity of significance which the matter had assumed in the poet's mind; and without this unity of significance, the expression of the matter would have been incomplete and crippled.[76]

[Conception] is the stage in which the inspiration of some imaginative experience completely establishes itself in the poet's mind, as an affair of clear imagery, vivid importance, and delightful excitement: also as a focus of varied and perhaps only just suggested associations and allusions; but above all as a single inclusive harmony, however complex, of all that it contains. Verbal art has no place in it. It may complete itself in an instant and without conscious effort; or it may be a gradual development and, in part at least, have been deliberately thought out. It certainly will have been this latter, if it is the conception of a dramatic or narrative poem, requiring a considerable organisation of parts; and in that case, no doubt, *verbal thought will have helped the process of conception* [my italics]. But only for the purpose of clarifying or developing the poet's own sense of what he wants to say, not for the purpose of saying it: only for the purpose of elaborating his imagination, not for the purpose of communicating it.

The art of poetry, however, does not exist until both stages have been accomplished. A man is not to be accounted a poet simply for being sensitive or excitable. A sunset may mean wonders to him; an old story may have fired his fancy into a rapture. But he is not a poet unless his wonders and raptures have ceased to be private to himself, and have become available to every one. A

75. *Ibid.*, p. 71. Bottomley draws the same distinction: "The sudden leap of intuitions and surmises, the magical way that light suddenly emanates from within something that we had previously and vainly endeavoured to illumine from without: these are the only foundation for true creation of beauty, and all else is useless if they are not vouchsafed. But to have them is only a third of the battle; and the remaining two-thirds are dogged hard work and illimitable patience." Letter from Gordon Bottomley to Paul Nash, dated April 14, 1910, in Claude C. Abbott and Anthony Bertram, eds., *Poet and Painter: Being the Correspondence between Gordon Bottomley and Paul Nash* (London, 1955), p. 2.

76. Abercrombie, *The Theory of Poetry*, pp. 73-74.

poet, that is to say, is not only a man of remarkable imaginative life, but a man who can express this.

Now expression is a somewhat ambiguous word. It means two quite different things in the two stages of poetic composition. This is what I want to stress in this lecture; *for otherwise the peculiar manners of poetic technique might seem a mere affair of traditional etiquette* [my italics]. In the stage of conception, an inspiration *expresses* itself by the mere fact of being unmistakably and vividly *known*. As soon as the poet is perfectly aware of his own experience — of all that can be seen and felt in it — of all that it is and all that it means to him — then, as far as he is concerned, expression is complete: the event, whatever it was, has expressed itself to him, and he has expressed himself, in his experience of it. But if a poem is to come of this, what happened in the poet's mind must somehow be made to happen in other minds: the image and its meaning must be conveyed to us. That is to say, some vehicle must be contrived to carry it. . . . So now begins the stage of technique: the stage in which something which does not exist as language — namely, an event in the poet's life — has to translate itself into an existence alien to its first nature: into the existence which is given by language. For not otherwise could it escape from the privacy of the poet's own mind; and it is . . . the essential thing in poetry, that imagination should thereby escape from the self-consciousness of the poet and become the property of the whole world.[77]

Here, then, in Abercrombie's terms, is the Georgian distinction between conception and technique; and it is markedly different from that form-content division that served to make possible the valuation of poems in relation to the "soundness" of their ideas. The Georgian distinction served, rather, to call attention to the special province of poetry — richly compelling, peculiarly intense moments of experience — and to the functional dependence of poets on the full resources of poetic language as the means of maximizing both their comprehension of experience and their ability to convey it. Since what poets seek to understand and to communicate is by its very nature subtle, complex, and elusive, mastery of language becomes an absolute condition of their enterprise. As poets, they must attempt simultaneously to extend their use of language in the interest of greater expressiveness and to

77. *Ibid.*, pp. 77-80. Here again Georgian and Imagist poetics agree more nearly than is commonly supposed. Hulme's sense of the relation between an "actual and vividly felt experience" and the art by which that experience is communicated directly comes close to Abercrombie's. Cf. Sections 21-28 of "Bergson's Theory of Art," in *Speculations*.

restrict their use of language in the interest of better communication. Everything rests upon their skill in resolving these opposed tendencies; for, as poets, the forms of language are the perfection of their experience. It was in this general sense that the Georgians were dedicated to craftsmanship, preoccupied with matters of form and technique, hostile to free verse: the right word must be chosen, words must be formed into the most appropriate structural patterns, and lines must be measured for possible amplifications of meaning.

It was this orientation, not pedantry or foppishness, that informed Marsh's strong preference for design and intelligibility in poetry. In extenuation of his view that some poems he had been asked to criticize were experimental to the point of formlessness and obscurity, Marsh wrote this letter in 1913:

> I warned you I was going to write in defence of my ideas about poetical expression. I don't think I made you understand them in the train, because you said I was "timorous," which could only mean that I was afraid of expression without authority and usage behind it. I don't think that is my failing, as I rejoice particularly in any bold and new use of language if I am satisfied that it really means what it is meant to mean, and also in any novelty of form if I find that it has and obeys a law of its own. I suppose we should agree that poetry *is* expression, and that if so it must have a meaning, and must convey it; and it seems to me that the "kritik" I was arguing upon in the train is a necessary deduction from those simple facts. . . . Do you know the story of one of the Symbolistes . . . who was writing a poem when a ray of sunlight fell upon his paper, and the word *palme* suddenly came into his head, so he put *palme* in the middle of his poem, hoping that it would convey his feeling about the sunlight to his readers? You will agree that this was going too far, but I thought your principles tended in that direction.[78]

Similarly, in citing the considerations that guided his selections for *Georgian Poetry*, Marsh stressed the functional basis of his insistence upon clarity as a poetic standard:

> "Intelligibility" is a relative term, and I naturally don't use it so as to exclude the poetry of suggestion; but I hold strongly that

---

78. Letter to Michael Sadleir, quoted in Hassall, *A Biography of Edward Marsh*, pp. 209-210.

poetry is communication, and that it is the poet's duty, to the best of his ability, to let the reader know what he is driving at. [79]

Marsh's emphasis on clarity as a criterion of poetic worth has too often been misunderstood as the sign of an unrealistic partiality to simple poetry. But his insistence upon clarity is more properly related to his philosophical orientation, which set a high value upon objective and precise transcription of complex experiential states and recognized poetic language as the most adequate means of transcribing them. We can derive some sense of Marsh's view of the relationship between conception and technique from Isaac Rosenberg, who was — while in the trenches in France — receiving his poetic education from Marsh. In a letter postmarked January 30, 1917, Rosenberg addressed Marsh thus:

> I think with you that poetry should be definite thought and clear expressions, however subtle; I don't think there should be any vagueness at all, but a sense of something hidden and felt to be there. Now, when my things fail to be clear, I am sure it is because of the luckless choice of a word or the failure to introduce a word that would flash my idea plain, as it is to my own mind. I believe my Amazon poem to be my best poem. If there is any difficulty, it must be in words here and there, the changing or elimination of which may make the poem clear. It has taken me about a year to write; for I have changed and rechanged it and thought hard over that poem, and striven to get that sense of inexorableness the human (or unhuman) side of this war has. It even penetrates behind human life. [80]

Surely, Moore and Russell would have acquiesced in Marsh's conviction that poetry, as a *kind* of communication, ought to aim for as much intelligibility as the conceptions it dealt with allowed. Too little form or too much formal eccentricity left the poet's conception too private to mean very much, while failure to be

79. Marsh, *A Number of People*, p. 322. De la Mare observes admiringly that Brooke's words "mean precisely what they say and only what they say," that his "world stands out sharp and distinct" (*Rupert Brooke and the Intellectual Imagination*, p. 16).

80. Isaac Rosenberg, quoted in "Introductory Memoir" by Laurence Binyon, in *Poems by Isaac Rosenberg*, ed. Gordon Bottomley (London, 1922), pp. 36-37. Abercrombie maintained that "the duty of a poet is so to precipitate his verbal thought as to cause an aura of non-verbal thought to cling about it: as a fine dust scattered in water vapour will, on settling, bring down with it a condensation of moisture" (*Speculative Dialogues*, p. 41). And Bottomley observed that "the greatest mystery comes by the greatest definiteness" (Abbott and Bertram, eds., *Poet and Painter*, p. 3).

sufficiently individual and creative in the employment of form —
that is, the undiscriminating reliance upon conventional forms —
masked the poet's conception in faceless generality. His vision was
to move beyond insignificant details without drifting into abstraction, and it was to disregard the conventional wisdom without
turning inward into subjectivism. The balance could be struck only
through the mastery of form, through the exploitation of every
linguistic resource and an absolute commitment to the importance
of revision. The results of this rigorous technical discipline, strictly
enforced by Marsh,[81] were poems so apparently unlabored, so
unrhetorical, so *clear*, that they have seemed to many critics
deficient in content. As Ross usefully reminds us, "at its best,
Georgian diction can be deceptive, for its very simplicity may
sometimes lull a reader into failing to recognize the high order of
technical mastery implied."[82]

In their choice of words, the Georgians set up transparency as
the ideal of the poetic craftsman. They sought to cultivate a
diction that did not call attention to itself — to either its modish-
ness or peculiarity — but which unobtrusively helped to *form* the
precise conception that the poet intended to communicate. To the
extent that diction achieved this end it was held to be "truthful."
Thus, the Georgians were not opposed to the use of archaic and
heavily figurative language out of any simple concern for artistic
verisimilitude; nor did they favor colloquial language because it
was more consistent with actual usage. They generally shunned the
former and inclined toward the latter because they wished to
employ a vocabulary within which it was possible to communicate
the truths residual in human experience. Much of the traditional
poetic vocabulary had worn too smooth, like old coins, had
become commonplace rhetorical gestures. Alternatively, if poetry
is an act of communication, the poet may not invent a sub-
stantially new vocabulary. Consequently, the Georgians regarded
colloquial language as most amenable to their purpose in that it

81. In this connection, it may be useful to refer to Lawrence's characterization of
Marsh as "a bit of a policeman in poetry" (letter to Marsh, postmarked November 19,
1913, in Moore, ed., *The Collected Letters of D. H. Lawrence*, I, 244). Although
Lawrence appears to have mistaken Marsh's fastidious concern over formal matters for
literary conventionalism, his designation of Marsh as a "policeman" is of some interest
within the context of my argument.
82. Ross, *The Georgian Revolt*, p. 125.

seemed to them to offer the greatest expressive possibilities. According to Abercrombie, "it is the common words that have the finest triumphs in poetry, because they necessarily have the greatest suggestive power behind them."[83] Yet, conscious of the need to exploit every usable resource of language in their effort to achieve both particularity and objectivity in poetry, the Georgians never abandoned archaisms and other traditional poetic locutions. They used them, albeit sparingly, whenever their use appeared functional:

> Of course, poets will always delight in rare or archaic or even dialect words — in anything which may increase the range of expression and give it some desired peculiarity.[84]

Brooke's "Fragment" and "The Great Lover"[85] reveal very well the Georgians' craftsmanlike employment of diction. The language is in no obvious way either poetic or colloquial; it seems purely referential, directing us — without deflection — to complex experiential states so intensely felt that their communication requires no other justification. In "Fragment," the speaker is contemplating companions soon to enter battle who do not yet give any sign of anticipating the destruction of war:

> I strayed about the deck, an hour, to-night
> Under a cloudy moonless sky; and peeped
> In at the windows, watched my friends at table,
> Or playing cards, or standing in the doorway,
> Or coming out into the darkness. Still
> No one could see me.

The speaker is then struck by the way in which he might predictably have responded to their heedlessness, and implies that he has been prevented from this:

> I would have thought of them
> — Heedless, within a week of battle — in pity,

83. Abercrombie, *The Theory of Poetry*, p. 138.

84. *Ibid.*, p. 138. Bottomley described the poetic use of language as the "level where language leaves behind its utilitarian purposes, and, in masterly hands, tends from every point of its circumference to the one central purpose of complete expression" ("Poetry and the Contemporary Theatre," in *Essays and Studies*, p. 139).

85. Keynes, ed., *The Poetical Works of Rupert Brooke*, pp. 17, 30-32.

> Pride in their strength and in the weight and firmness
> And link'd beauty of bodies, and pity that
> This gay machine of splendour'ld soon be broken,
> Thought little of, pashed, scattered. . . .

The final stanza introduces the speaker's larger awareness of human vulnerability, his sense that the insubstantiality of their lives derives from a material principle more fundamental than war:

> Only, always,
> I could but see them — against the lamplight — pass
> Like coloured shadows, thinner than filmy glass,
> Slight bubbles, fainter than the wave's faint light,
> That broke to phosphorus out in the night,
> Perishing things and strange ghosts — soon to die
> To other ghosts — this one, or that, or I.

The language of the first stanza approaches prose in its flat colloquialness, in its obvious determination to avoid being poetic. Its bareness serves to endow the dramatic situation with an incontrovertible existence; its understatedness suggests that only the elemental details of the experience have been provided, that no gratuitous elaboration is present. In the second stanza, the tone is altered by the introduction of the poetic phrases "link'd beauty of bodies" and "gay machine of splendour" and the counterpointing of those phrases with the dialect word "pashed." These contrasting verbal expansions of tone convey precisely the pity of heroic beauty brutally smashed without regard for its fineness, a response that is made to seem *both* appropriate and irrelevant by the speaker's selection of the verb "would" in the first line of this stanza. The more densely figurative language of the third stanza signals another shift in the speaker's tone. The intuitive sense of a world so fluid and wavering that even its most palpable forms may be conceived as shadows and ghosts forces the speaker to express through a sequence of analogies his vision of human frailty. It is this figurative illumination of the world's essential ghostliness that has emptied the speaker of his capacity to pity his companions in the terms of conventional sentiment. But these employments of diction force no conclusion upon the reader. Rather, the precision with which language is handled conveys the conception so resonantly and faithfully that the reader is entirely absorbed in the

experience itself. Monro testified to the presence of the same skill
in one of the lesser known Georgians, Ralph Hodgson:

> While most poets glean their vocabulary from poetry itself, this
> one gathers his, as it were, raw from life. . . . Reading him we
> think: Here is a man who talks only a language of his own, and
> with such native purity does he use this tongue he knows so well,
> that he never utters a word of it in a wrong sense, nor fails to
> make himself clearly understood.[86]

The Georgians extended their insistence upon maximal transparency and expressiveness in lexical choice to their consideration
of syntax. Here too they avoided the extremes of literary convention, as in positional inversions, and of excessive novelty, as in
massive departures from standard English word order. Abercrombie offers this account of the nature and function of syntax
in poetry:

> What holds good of words and phrases, holds good too of syntax.
> If there is such a thing as poetic syntax, it is the syntax of
> language spoken. But the argument need hardly be carried fur-
> ther. Think only of the extraordinary expressiveness gained in
> spoken English from the order of the words in a sentence; here
> we come on something like the values of words as distinct from
> their obvious meaning: but now it is the value of a whole
> sentence of meaning, changeable according as the order of the
> words may be changed without loss of logical force. No poet who
> knows his business will neglect so fine a means of conveying
> shades of significance. But on the whole the structure of thought
> in language does not offer such scope for exceptional, immediate
> expressiveness as the diction which builds up that structure; we
> naturally look for poetic quality in words and idioms rather than
> in the planning of sentences, the quality of which has no great
> range of variation. The chief importance of syntax in poetry is of
> another order. It is not remarkably concerned with the actual
> symbolising of imaginative experience which we call *poetry*; it is
> rather concerned with the organisation of this business into
> *poems*. The intellectual shape of poetical matter — the coherent
> isolation of it into self-sufficient organism — to effect *that* is the
> affair of syntax in poetry. Without it, we could never know the
> real significance of poetic detail.[87]

86. Monro, *Some Contemporary Poets*, p. 67.
87. Abercrombie, *The Theory of Poetry*, pp. 146-147.

The syntax of Brooke's "Fragment" is carefully shaped into two complete sentences; and the second sentence clearly frames the speaker's dilemma by not only bridging his projected and actual response to the prospect of death, but by showing how one is related to the other: "I would have thought of them/ . . . in pity/ . . . Only, always."

In the same spirit, the Georgians extended their sense of the vital function of form in poetry to the metering of the lines:

> For what metre effects cannot possibly be expressed by anything but metre itself: that, in fact, is just why metre is so invaluable to the poet.[88]

Versification was not to be practiced mechanically, as a demonstration of facility or as a concession to poetic tradition and public taste.[89] Rather, properly managed, it might extend the poet's expressive powers — always severely taxed by the distinctive function of poetry — and permit him to verbalize with greater particularity the total character of his conception. Brooke summarizes the point admirably:

> There are certain extremely valuable "aesthetic" feelings to be got through literature. These can be got, it is empirically certain, sometimes through prose, of the ordinary and of the Whitmanic kind, often and more intensely through poetry, in which the three elements of thought, words, and metre are employed.[90]

In "Fragment" the use of unrhymed and enjambed but regularly iambic lines in the first stanza helps to establish its tonal quality of elemental concreteness, its studied lack of elaboration. The meter is varied in the second stanza by the absence of caesura in the third and fifth lines, producing an unchecked flow of language that helps the diction to communicate breath-taking magnificence soon to be smashed. In the third stanza, the speaker is wrestling with the task of articulating the intuitively or imaginatively appre-

---

88. Abercrombie, *Poetry: Its Music and Meaning*, p. 41.

89. Bottomley, for example, argued that dramatic poetry "must learn again to base itself upon contemporary speech-rhythms . . . upon, that is, contemporary sound, and not either the look of a printed page or even a bygone usage of sound" ("Poetry and the Contemporary Theatre," in *Essays and Studies*, pp. 141-142).

90. Christopher Hassall, ed., *The Prose of Rupert Brooke* (London, 1956), p. 112.

hended principle of man's generic frailty; and here the meter is strained by a significant number of substitutions and by the way in which the semantic stresses play against the metrical requirements, amplifying the strained quality of the intensely figurative diction. It is also significant that in this stanza, where the speaker struggles to express the perception that has overshadowed his pity, the poet extends his employment of poetic form by making his only use of rhyme in the poem. In other words, the Georgians recognized that by modifying a formal metrical pattern with other prosodic devices they could produce rhythmic variations in poetic speech that might both echo and enlarge the expressiveness of their diction.

The special character of the early Georgians' interest in form and craftsmanship inclined them toward narrative and dramatic poetry and away from the lyric, especially from such genteel performances as the occasional odes much affected by popular poets like William Watson. The Georgians had a definite predilection for the ballad, with its tradition of objective narration and honest colloquial diction. The ballad seemed to them one of the forms particularly amenable to the communication of poetic truth, and the Georgians were accordingly in the vanguard of the ballad revival in contemporary poetry.

I have denominated exacting craftsmanship and concern for form the last principle of the Georgian poetic because it can only be understood in the context of the first three principles. These three principles made indefatigable attention to the fourth principle the ultimate test of the poet. They gave the refinement of technique its crucial function and made the poet's absolute mastery of his craft obligatory. It was from this vantage point that the Georgians deplored the technique of many of their late Victorian and Modernist contemporaries. They were equally opposed to encrusted forms and formlessness, to meaningless convention and meaningless revolt. Thus, on the one hand, the Georgians manifested what Edmund Gosse called an "almost crazy fear" of rhetoric,[91] of inflated and magniloquent language, which they condemned as pompous and fraudulent:

91. Quoted in Hassall. *A Biography of Edward Marsh,* pp. 501-502.

> The temporary reputation acquired by Mr. Watson is particularly
> pernicious to the well-being of Poetry; and it is ridiculous as well
> as aggravating that any notice should be taken of his pompous
> outcries.[92]

On the other hand, they were outraged by the apparent misunderstanding of the nature and purpose of art that disposed a rapidly
increasing number of poets to experiment feverishly in an effort to
compose with greater individuality. These proponents of a personal art often departed completely from the conventional forms
either to create new ones or to overturn the idea of form itself. It
was about the time of the founding of *Georgian Poetry* that free
verse was first practiced in England, and Marsh was adamant in his
opposition to its use. In this connection, Brooke judged Whitman
a "dangerous influence."[93] Flecker spoke against the use of free
verse,[94] Abercrombie thought meter "incomparably more suited
to the purposes of poetry than free rhythm,"[95] and — excepting
only D. H. Lawrence — the other early Georgians were of the same
mind. Even Harold Monro, the Georgian most receptive to the
Modernist position, had his reservations about free verse.[96] Consequently, whether they looked to the right or to the left, the
Georgians saw poetic form misused or ignored, to the unfailing
disadvantage of poetry.

There were, however, a few somewhat neglected elder poets,
conspicuous for their independence and dedication to poetry,
whom the Georgians acknowledged as true poets and honored.
Marsh held Robert Bridges in very great esteem, and the following
comment by Monro helps to explain why the first volume of
Georgian Poetry was dedicated to Bridges:

> Mr. Robert Bridges, we are told, accepted the Laureateship on his
> own terms, and it is certain that, in his almost complete absten-
> tion from the composition of ceremonial odes, or of artificial
> complimentary poems, as by his continued concentration on the
> theory and practice of his own proper art, he has restored much

---

92. Flecker, *Collected Prose*, p. 218.
93. Hassall, *The Prose of Rupert Brooke*, p. 112.
94. Goldring, *James Elroy Flecker*, p. 68.
95. Abercrombie, *The Theory of Poetry*, pp. 171-173.
96. Monro, *Some Contemporary Poets*, p. 105.

dignity to the office, besides adding a significance which it had not previously possessed.[97]

A. E. Housman was held in like esteem by the Georgians. He was invited by Marsh to contribute to the first volume of *Georgian Poetry*,[98] Brooke quoted him "with approval,"[99] and Monro pronounced *A Shropshire Lad* "the antithesis of that bulky pomposity of late Victorianism."[100] Profoundly dissatisfied with the waxlike poetry of doctrine and rhetorical mannerism, the Georgians appreciated Housman's use of the ballad form, with its sturdy common speech and genuine feeling and its objective mode of presentation. Further, "Housman's manuscripts testify to his unremitting effort to secure the precise effect intended, and every emendation proves the infallibility of his instinct for the right word."[101] And the Georgians readily appreciated carefully wrought diction and general poetic craftsmanship. Monro offered this assessment of Housman's style:

> It shows the greatest forbearance, containing not a word too many and revealing a complete resistance to the common temptation to add ornament, the yielding to which has ruined the style of so many a lesser poet. It conveys the appearance of ease, and the feeling of vigour. It is truly a style: not a *manner*. Lastly, where it includes poetical devices or the use of inversion, these are so discriminatingly managed as to render them either unobtrusive, or else noticeably and characteristically proper to their context.[102]

But the elder contemporary most universally respected by the Georgians was Thomas Hardy, to whom Marsh dedicated the fourth volume of *Georgian Poetry*:

> One great, unfashionable figure inspired many of the Georgian poets: Thomas Hardy. He had always been aloof from fashions in

97. *Ibid.*, pp. 34-35. According to Sir Henry Newbolt, by 1897 Bridges was urging "the great need of modern poetry for a fresher diction and a broader freedom." Sir Henry Newbolt, *My World as in My Time* (London, 1932), p. 194.

98. See Hassall, *A Biography of Edward Marsh*, pp. 189, 191, 194.

99. Keynes, "Preface," *The Poetical Works of Rupert Brooke*, p. 8.

100. Monro, *Some Contemporary Poets*, p. 18.

101. Joseph Warren Beach, "The Literature of the Nineteenth and the Early Twentieth Centuries, 1798 to the First World War," in *A History of English Literature*, ed. Hardin Craig (New York, 1950), p. 588.

102. Monro, *Some Contemporary Poets*, p. 49..

verse, and cannot be fitted tidily into any "movement" but what made him attractive was his love for the English countryside and English tradition, combined with the gnarled honesty of his mind and verse, and the spirit of high, anguished doubt about man's and the world's destiny in his heart.[103]

The Georgians were perhaps most drawn to what has been called the "elemental vision" [104] of Hardy's poetry. In the "Apology" prefixed to *Late Lyrics and Earlier*, Hardy asserted that what was alleged to be his "pessimism" was, in fact, merely " 'questionings' in the exploration of reality." [105] Speaking as an "evolutionary meliorist," he insisted that his readers must see the world as it is and at its worst, if there was to be any meaningful discussion of human improvement. F. R. Leavis has characterized Hardy's poetic vision in this way:

> Hardy's greatness lies in the integrity with which he accepted the conclusion . . . that nature is indifferent to human values, in the completeness of his recognition, and in the purity and adequacy of his response. He was betrayed into no heroic postures. He felt deeply and consistently, he knew what he felt, and, in his best poems, communicated it perfectly.[106]

Hardy did not merely versify his reflections or his "philosophy," says Leavis; he was, rather, compelled by the intensity of his remembered experience to write as he did.[107] Hardy wrote neither dutifully nor obediently; he wrote as though he was compelled by experience to give it an honest report, whatever that might entail. Unlike J. M. Barrie, Hardy would not gratify the desires of his audience for sentiment and approved moral doctrine; and he had, accordingly, suffered its hostility. One of the sources of Hardy's appeal to the Georgians may have been his turning away from the writing of prose to the full-time practice of poetry after the reception of *Jude the Obscure* in 1895. The turn to poetry could thus be viewed as signaling his absolute determina-

103. G. S. Fraser, *The Modern Writer and His World* (London, 1953), p. 198.
104. R. L. Mégroz, *Modern English Poetry: 1882-1932* (London, 1933), p. 72.
105. Thomas Hardy, *Collected Poems* (New York, 1943), p. 526.
106. F. R. Leavis, *New Bearings in English Poetry* (London, 1950), p. 58.
107. *Ibid.*, pp. 60-61.

tion not to compromise his literary independence; it was his renunciation of any possibility of large public acceptance. Coming when it did, fifteen years before their own repudiation of public literary taste, Hardy's gesture must have struck the Georgians as a particularly courageous one. In addition to admiring this rare dedication to poetry, the Georgians were favorably impressed with Hardy's celebrated awkwardness of expression. For the Georgians, this was the formal equivalent of his intellectual honesty; it revealed that Hardy was more drawn to the relation of truth than to the achievement of magniloquence.

Despite his own poetic practice,[108] Sir Henry Newbolt earned the appreciation of the Georgians for his efforts in behalf of the new poetry. As the editor of *The Monthly Review* from 1900 to 1904, Newbolt published poetry by Hardy and Bridges; and he was among the first to champion de la Mare's poetry. He presided over the opening ceremonies of the Poetry Bookshop; and, as a frequent lecturer for the Royal Society of Literature, he expressed — albeit cautiously — his support of the Marsh circle:

> I even ventured to speak with conviction of younger men, of the "Georgians" as we called them, in a room where a dozen of them were standing clustered together on the outside of the well-packed circle: and I remember a letter from their editor, Edward Marsh, in which he set forth the dates of my lectures and of his successive editions in a very flattering parallel. Rupert Brooke, Walter de la Mare and Ralph Hodgson also wrote to the same effect, and helped me to believe my effort worth making.[109]

Among American poets contemporary with them, the Georgians singled out only Robert Frost and Edwin Arlington Robinson as praiseworthy. Gibson and Abercrombie proclaimed Frost's merits, and Brooke discovered Robinson's poetry during his American travels in 1913. He wrote to Monro that Robinson was the "One poet" that he had found in America, and promised to "boom

---

108. See chapter 3 above.

109. Margaret Newbolt, ed., *The Later Life and Letters of Sir Henry Newbolt* (London, 1942), pp. 163, 217. See also Joy Grant, *Harold Monro and the Poetry Bookshop* (London, 1967), pp. 56-57, 62-63. For evidence of Newbolt's receptiveness to experiment in poetry, see his *A New Study of English Poetry* (London, 1917), pp. 42-43, 111-113, 240-241.

him" upon his return to England. A month later, in a letter to Gosse, he observed that Robinson's "queer kind of intimacy with the small objects and affairs of life" and his "musical power over common words and phrases" were akin to de la Mare's.[110]

110. Keynes, ed., *The Letters of Rupert Brooke*, pp. 473, 494. An aversion to rhetoric, doctrinizing, and conventional poetic diction together with a disposition to present ideas and states of mind in dramatic form were central tenets of Robinson's "poetic." See Wallace L. Anderson, "The Young Robinson as Critic and Self-Critic," in *Edwin Arlington Robinson: Centenary Essays*, ed. Ellsworth Barnard (Athens, Ga., 1969), pp. 68-87.

5

CONCLUSION

Although Marsh eschewed manifestoes, he and his circle of Georgians possessed a poetic whose origins lay in the philosophical ambience of Cambridge during the 1890s. That poetic informed the first two volumes of *Georgian Poetry*; but it was partly obscured by the introduction of the young Georgian war poets and the nucleus of the Squire group into the third volume, and it was almost wholly displaced from the last two volumes, which became episodes in the open warfare between John Squire and the Modernists. This change in the composition of *Georgian Poetry* was not the result of a cleverly managed Neo-Georgian coup. It occurred because both Marsh and his Georgians accepted it quite passively, neither welcoming nor opposing it. They seem, rather, merely to have relaxed their hold and allowed circumstances to rule. Some of the early Georgians had grown uneasy over the flourishing sales and wide celebrity of the first two volumes; and since each succeeding volume was intended to publish work written since the preceding one, it was possible for them to demur gently, to speak of having nothing new or nothing suitable, and to encourage Marsh to look to newer poets unknown as they to the public before the first volume of *Georgian Poetry*.[1] While they continued to honor Marsh's insistent requests, they did so with diminished enthusiasm. For his part, Marsh was a busy civil servant closely involved in the career of Winston Churchill. In

---

1. For example, although de la Mare continued to contribute to *Georgian Poetry*, it was at Marsh's prodding. In response to Marsh's request that he contribute to the fifth volume, de la Mare contended that the third volume was the last in which he had appropriately appeared. In a letter to de la Mare in 1922 dealing with the preparation of the fifth volume, Marsh noted that "several of the old stagers are dropping out." Christopher Hassall, *A Biography of Edward Marsh* (New York, 1959), pp. 493-494.

February 1921, for example, Churchill became Colonial Secretary, with the settlement of Home Rule for Ireland as his most pressing task. As Churchill's secretary, Marsh was deeply preoccupied with this and other matters; and his literary interests were accordingly set aside for a time. Thus, when Marsh was informed by Monro in 1921 that a fifth volume of *Georgian Poetry* was in demand, he proposed an extended delay.[2] And so when Squire — an early ally as literary editor of the *New Statesman* and a critic whose reputation had risen sharply during the war years — offered his leadership and extraordinary vigor, *Georgian Poetry* altered its course.

There had been disagreements with Pound and other Modernists as early as 1913; but the mutual opposition of Georgian and Modernist to the late Victorians, the broad range of Marsh's literary friendships, and his disinclination for public debate all served to prevent escalation.[3] As a longtime professional journalist, however, Squire was quite ready to engage Pound, Eliot, Middleton Murry, and the Sitwells in open exchange. His general inhospitality to the Modernist program antedated his inclusion, together with his protégés John Freeman and W. J. Turner, in the third volume of *Georgian Poetry*; but the Modernist critique of that volume and its two successors clearly added to his readiness for combat. Moreover, Squire's Cambridge liberalism had undergone a change during the war years. He felt increasingly committed to an older England, and accordingly began to fight a rear-guard action against those who would "make it new." What he took to be the formlessness and unintelligibility of Modernist poets like the Sitwells and Eliot aroused his moral indignation. Consequently, like the tory satirists of the eighteenth century, Squire cast himself in the role of Horatius at the bridge and resolved to oppose the descent of English poetry into chaos and night.

2. *Ibid.*, p. 487.
3. It seems clear that Marsh fundamentally shared Squire's reservations about Modernist poetry, but his only open provocation of the Modernists was the "Prefatory Note" to the final volume of *Georgian Poetry*: "Much admired modern work seems to me, in its lack of inspiration and its disregard of form, like gravy imitating lava." But even here he genially conceded that the Modernists might correspondingly find the work he preferred, "in its lack of inspiration and its comparative finish, like tapioca imitating pearls." And he tactfully concluded that "Either view — possibly both — may be right." *Georgian Poetry: 1920-1922* (London, 1922).

Although Squire had become a socialist during his undergraduate years at Cambridge and remained a radical during his early career as a journalist in Plymouth and London, and although he became a regular contributor to A. R. Orage's guild socialist weekly, the *New Age* (where he approvingly reviewed Pound's *Canzoni*), and in 1913 was selected by Sidney and Beatrice Webb as the literary editor of their new Fabian weekly, the *New Statesman*,[4] he had shifted heavily toward toryism by 1919 when he became an indisputable literary power as editor of the *London Mercury*. In seeking to account for Squire's gradual shift from the socialist aestheticism he espoused in 1913, one may point to the great impact of the war upon him. Unable to serve owing to poor eyesight, he came to feel what his biographer calls "a comprehensive, perhaps even an exaggerated, respect for those who had taken part in active service." During the war years, he grew more critical of obscenity and obscurity in literature. And by 1917, when Squire was elevated to the editorship of the *New Statesman*, he had become — by his own testimony and Arnold Bennett's — patriotic and even jingoistic.[5] Another conservatizing influence upon Squire was his friendship with Edmund Gosse, who by 1918 had come to regard Squire as his successor as chief literary arbiter of English public taste. Gosse "arranged Squire's election as a member of the National Club . . . in order that they might have a common meeting-ground," and was mainly responsible for Squire's election in 1919 as a fellow of the Royal Society of Literature.[6]

Squire's first relationship with Marsh's Georgian circle had been strangely divided despite the Cambridge connection. As literary editor of the *New Statesman* (whose inception in April 1913 closely followed the launching of *Georgian Poetry*), he displayed early support of the Marsh circle by favorably reviewing the first volume of *Georgian Poetry* and by promptly championing the poetry of de la Mare, Bottomley, Brooke, Davies, Gibson, Flecker, and Lawrence — some of whom he had published in the *New*

4. Patrick Howarth, *Squire: "Most Generous of Men"* (London, 1963), pp. 39-42, 50-53, 63-66, 69, 72-73, 77-78.

5. *Ibid.*, pp. 93, 109, 114.

6. *Ibid.*, p. 117.

Statesman at Marsh's urging.[7] But Squire was critical of the second volume's brand of realism, which he pronounced excessive and artificial as employed in the poetic dramas of Bottomley and Abercrombie; and several of the Georgians responded by professing small regard for Squire's abilities as a critic of poetry.[8] Moreover, like Marsh, Squire was a discoverer and patron of poets, so that if he was responsive to Marsh's urgings that he publish certain Georgians in the *New Statesman*, he in turn championed the work of John Freeman, W. J. Turner, and Edward Shanks and urged Marsh to publish them in *Georgian Poetry*. Thus, there was enough manifest and latent tension in the relations between the Marsh and Squire circles to make the inclusion of Squire, Freeman, and Turner in the third volume of *Georgian Poetry* immediately problematic.

Squire's appointment as editor of a new monthly, the *London Mercury*, greatly enlarged the power he had possessed as editor of the *New Statesman* and deepened his influence upon the editorial policy of *Georgian Poetry*. He now had the authority and freedom to do what he pleased; and he undertook, through the *London Mercury* and the last two volumes of *Georgian Poetry*, to shape postwar writing in England. The Squire group in *Georgian Poetry* was increased by the addition of Edward Shanks and Francis Brett-Young to the fourth volume and of Edmund Blunden and Martin Armstrong to the fifth. And the first number of the *London Mercury* in November 1919 announced Squire's decision to provide a counterstatement to Modernism in the arts, to oppose unintelligibility and self-indulgent experimentation. By the time of the appearance of the last volume of *Georgian Poetry* in 1922 and his condemnatory review of *The Waste Land* in 1923, Squire had set the term "Georgian" definitively into a new posture. For the next generation, it was commonly understood to refer to a dead literary movement fixedly hostile to contemporary reality and to

7. *Ibid.*, pp. 87, 91.
8. Robert H. Ross, *The Georgian Revolt, 1910-1922* (Carbondale, Ill., 1965), pp. 134-136. In his attempt to convince Squire of the merits of *King Lear's Wife*, Marsh argued that Squire "was criticizing art by ethical standards." Hassall, *A Biography of Edward Marsh*, p. 378. Squire also parodied the poetry of both Masefield and Davies. See J. C. Squire, *Tricks of the Trade* (London, 1917); and Herbert Palmer, *Post-Victorian Poetry* (London, 1938), pp. 197-200.

new ways of constituting that reality. Further, given Squire's absolute commitment to publishing his friends and advancing their careers, it was also understood to refer to a self-serving clique, the "Squirearchy."[9] Squire's service as a judge of the Hawthornden Prize who awarded it to members of his own circle became an infamous example of his partisanship.

As this shift in the term's meaning occurred, some members of the early Georgian circle were concerned to distinguish the old stage of Georgianism from the new. Harold Monro commented disparagingly on the Neo-Georgian school and pointed directly to Squire's role in the formation of the second stage.[10] And Robert Graves, who had been discovered by Marsh while still a schoolboy in 1913 and carefully educated by Marsh in the principles of Georgian poetry, protested the emergence of the second stage and proposed that Marsh at least reflect this obvious division by arranging the contributors to the fifth volume into two categories: "the excellent Abercrombie – Hodgson – de la Mare – Brooke tradition of early Georgianism" and "this sham-Georgian school."[11]

By the same token, the Modernists contemporary with the Georgians were usually quite specific about which Georgians they were attacking; and it was the Squire group – not Marsh and his founding circle – upon whom their guns were trained. It was Squire, predictably, who ridiculed Wyndham Lewis, Pound, and Vorticism; and, as Howarth observes, for this opposition "he was not to be forgiven in certain quarters." It was Squire again who, in the first number of the *London Mercury* – with his editorial notes and a destructive review of Osbert Sitwell's experimental poetry – issued a "challenge to battle which was to be taken up with vigour by an unusually united family."[12] Squire pitted his *London Mercury* against the Sitwells's *Wheels* and Middleton Murry's

9. Howarth, *Squire: "Most Generous of Men,"* p. 146.

10. Harold Monro, *Some Contemporary Poets* (London, 1920), pp. 24-25, 149-151, 156.

11. Hassall, *A Biography of Edward Marsh*, p. 494. The critique of the Georgians by Laura Riding and Robert Graves in *A Survey of Modernist Poetry* (London, 1927) is properly read as an indictment of Neo-Georgian poetry, although some of Graves's commentators have read it as his repudiation of *all* Georgian poetry. See, for example, Michael Kirkham, *The Poetry of Robert Graves* (London, 1969), p. 29.

12. Howarth, *Squire: "Most Generous of Men,"* pp. 110-111, 124-129.

Athenaeum. Accordingly, under Murry's editorship following the war, the *Athenaeum* became one of the severest critics of the Georgians. But it was the Squire group who were Murry's targets, for Murry felt differently about Marsh to whom he had been introduced in 1912 by Brooke. Indeed, Marsh had been the patron of Murry's *Rhythm*, which for a time was "a vehicle for Georgian criticism."[13] The two most famous satires on Georgian poetry were aimed directly at Squire. First published in September 1922, Osbert Sitwell's "The Jolly Old Squire" satirized the mincing pastoralism and the venality of the Squire group, mediocre nature poets dedicated only to advancing their careers. In the poem, Squire is specifically charged with awarding literary prizes and reviews to his own friends. Roy Campbell's "The Georgiad," published a decade later in 1933, conceives Georgianism broadly enough to include the epicene world of Bloomsbury. But when Campbell isolates the type of the Georgian poet, it is Squire who is the central figure – a weekend rusticizer with a highly commercialized interest in melancholy subjects.[14] It was, therefore, the second stage of Georgian poetry that incurred the wrath and contempt of the Modernists; and that distinction was recognized as long as the conflict raged and Squire occupied the foreground. The distinction between Georgian and Neo-Georgian poets was drawn by Alec Waugh, Middleton Murry, and several other periodical critics of the early twenties; and it was elaborated by Herbert Palmer.[15] But by the thirties it was ignored or forgotten by critics and historians of modern poetry, and it became usual to conceive of Georgian poetry in general in terms of the characteristics of the Neo-Georgians as they were portrayed in Modernist polemics.[16]

Marsh's early Georgian group was not simply in retreat from the modern world to an uncomplicated Romantic countryside, as too many commentators have alleged. Nor were the Georgians, as

13. Hassall, *A Biography of Edward Marsh*, p. 188.

14. Osbert Sitwell, "The Jolly Old Squire," *The Collected Satires and Poems of Osbert Sitwell* (London, 1931), pp. 92-103; Roy Campbell, "The Georgiad," *The Collected Poems of Roy Campbell* (London, 1949), I, 201-242.

15. Ross, *The Georgian Revolt*, pp. 266, 273; Palmer, *Post-Victorian Poetry*, pp. 181-206.

16. About twenty years after Palmer, the distinction was revived in Hassall's *Biography of Edward Marsh* (see, for example, p. 683); in C. K. Stead's *The New Poetic* (London, 1964), pp. 93, 110, 189; and, most authoritatively, in Ross's *The Georgian Revolt* (see, for example, pp. 152-153, 162, 165).

others have argued, merely a rather weak, programless compromise between an exhausted Victorianism and the advance guard of Modernism.[17] Marsh's Georgians were not only in agreement about what constituted poetic error; they were also in agreement on what was taken to be the true nature and practice of poetry. In that understanding, no poetic manifesto was required or deemed desirable. But they shared a common discipline sufficiently to be able to exemplify a clear alternative to the more tendentious expressions of both Victorianism and Modernism, on the one hand, and of Neo-Georgianism, on the other.

One interesting consequence of a fuller understanding of the Georgian poetic is that several writers who have been exculpated by admiring critics from Georgian membership may now be seen more clearly. The very characteristics which critics have isolated in de la Mare, Davies, Edward Thomas, and Graves as the redeeming tokens of their distinction from the Georgians now appear to be consistent with a proper understanding of the Georgian movement. Thus, approving critics of poets typically associated with the Georgians have denied this relationship by singling out qualities that obviously do not accord with the conventional view of Georgian poetry; but the qualities that they have isolated as more fittingly descriptive are, in fact, quite often entirely consistent with a corrected account of the Georgian poetic. For example, the same critics who describe the Georgians as superficial lyrical escapists express their admiration for Ralph Hodgson in terms that are really applicable to virtually all the early Georgians:

> He is, one feels, a poet of complete integrity, who would only write when he had something he urgently wished to say; and who takes care to say it in the best possible way.[18]

And after declaring Edward Thomas "an original poet of rare quality, who has been associated with the Georgians by mischance," F. R. Leavis characterizes his work in a way that suggests its full harmony with the Georgian conception of realism:

17. For the view that Georgian poetry was a poetry of compromise, see H. N. Fairchild, *Religious Trends in English Poetry* (New York, 1962), V, 348-349.

18. Edith C. Batho and Bonamy Dobrée, *The Victorians and After* (London, 1950), p. 72.

A characteristic poem of his has the air of being a random jotting down of chance impressions and sensations, the record of a moment of relaxed and undirected consciousness. The diction and movement are those of quiet, ruminative speech. But the unobtrusive signs accumulate, and finally one is aware that the outward scene is accessory to an inner theatre. Edward Thomas is concerned with the finer texture of living, the here and now, the ordinary moments, in which for him the "meaning" (if any) resides. It is as if he were trying to catch some shy intuition on the edge of consciousness that would disappear if looked at directly.[19]

Similarly, after John Danby states as his initial premise that, despite "surface similarities" with the Georgians, "Thomas is really isolated in his time," he provides an account of Thomas's poetry that actually goes far toward explaining why de la Mare was so anxious to have Marsh include Thomas in *Georgian Poetry* that he offered to step down from the anthology to make place for him:

His poetry . . . becomes a subtle record of something in the texture of experience itself. . . .

Thomas's poetry is a valid exploration, not the exploitation of a mood or point of view. It states the realities of a constricted but centrally important area of experience. It strips itself naked of mannerism and attitudinising. The borrowed posture as well as the unfelt word is a betrayal.[20]

In his "Foreword" to Thomas's *Collected Poems*, de la Mare noted Thomas's "complete freedom of mind" and "love of truth," his unwillingness as a poet to be "all things to *all* men," and his detestation of "mere cleverness." "This is not," de la Mare said, "a poetry that will drug or intoxicate, civicise or edify — in the usual meaning of the word, though it rebuilds reality." Telling of "common experience," Thomas's "long-looking" poems "win at last to the inmost being of a thing."[21]

19. F. R. Leavis, *New Bearings in English Poetry* (London, 1950), pp. 66, 69.

20. John F. Danby, "Edward Thomas," *Critical Quarterly*, 1 (Winter 1959), 308, 310, 317. For an explanation of the circumstances behind Marsh's failure to include Thomas in *Georgian Poetry*, see Hassall, *A Biography of Edward Marsh*, pp. 211, 422; cf. William Cooke, *Edward Thomas: A Critical Biography* (London, 1970), pp. 92-93.

21. Walter de la Mare, "Foreword," *Collected Poems by Edward Thomas* (London, 1936), pp. 5, 9, 10. First published in 1920.

Like Thomas and Davies, Robert Graves has attracted admiring critics intent upon dissociating his literary reputation from that of the Georgians in order better to reveal his individual poetic achievement. This motive is evident in Douglas Day's remarks prefatory to his enthusiastic, vindicative study of Graves's poetic career:

> Most scholars (especially those on this side of the Atlantic) have persisted in linking him with such lesser fry as Edmund Blunden, Walter de la Mare, W. H. Davies, and the other contributors to the volumes of *Georgian Poetry* edited from 1911 to 1922 by Edward Marsh. That Graves, like D. H. Lawrence, did not tarry long in the Georgian camp has not apparently registered very strongly in academic circles.[22]

But, dependably, the qualities singled out by friendly critics as truly characteristic of Graves's individual poetic achievement are demonstrably Georgian, in the revised sense in which I use that term. For example, J. M. Cohen, after noting that Graves had "become an anti-Georgian" by about 1920, thus describes the poem that he takes to be the first reflection of Graves's "true manner":

> The course that Graves appears now to have set himself was towards increasing accuracy of vision and complexity of thought, expressed in the simplest and most economical way. He was addicted to no special vocabulary; he drew on the full resources of language.[23]

Other critics have regularly called attention to Graves's claim for the distinctive function of poetry, to his dedication to that function, to his poetic independence, and to his insistence upon form without their displaying any knowledge that these convictions were the very essence of the early Georgian program.

As these examples suggest, the historical and critical commentary on virtually all the poets linked to the first stage of Georgian poetry invites revision and amplification. Like their nearest American analogues, Robinson and Frost, the chief Georgian poets have too long been read by deputy, when they

---

22. Douglas Day, *Swifter Than Reason* (Chapel Hill, 1963), p. xii.
23. J. M. Cohen, *Robert Graves* (New York, 1961), pp. 21, 24.

have not gone entirely unread. Like Frost before Randall Jarrell, they await their "compleat" critics. The collected poems of Bottomley, Brooke, Abercrombie, Davies, de la Mare, Graves, and Thomas require a reading at once synoptic and connected; for the *Georgian Poetry* anthologies are not conterminous with Georgian poetry, which both antedated and survived them. Always independent and wary of group recognition, the Georgian poets regarded the success of Marsh's anthologies as an unexpected benefaction. Grateful as they were for the royalty earnings that Marsh carefully divided among them, by the time of the third volume in 1917 most of them contributed principally out of friendship for Marsh. Georgian poetry, as Marsh and Brooke conceived it, survives less in the first two or three *Georgian Poetry* anthologies than in the works of those poets who were indispensable to that conception.

SELECTED BIBLIOGRAPHY

Editions and compilations are listed under the editor's name to give prominence in this list to the scholarship on the Georgians. Important editions of Brooke's work, for example, are to be found under Marsh, Hassall, and Keynes — the better to stress the sources of our knowledge of the Georgians.

Abbott, Claude C. and Anthony Bertram, eds. *Poet and Painter: Being the Correspondence between Gordon Bottomley and Paul Nash.* London, 1955.

Abercrombie, Lascelles. *An Essay towards a Theory of Art.* London, 1922.

————. *Poetry: Its Music and Meaning.* London, 1932.

————. *Speculative Dialogues.* New York, 1913.

————. *The Theory of Poetry.* London, 1924.

Ayer, A. J. *Russell and Moore: The Analytical Heritage.* London, 1971.

Bottomley, Gordon. *Poems and Plays.* London, 1953.

————. *Poems of Thirty Years.* London, 1925.

Bottomley, Gordon, ed. *Poems by Isaac Rosenberg.* London, 1922.

Broad, C. D. "The Local Historical Background of Contemporary Cambridge Philosophy," in *British Philosophy in the Mid-Century: A Cambridge Symposium,* ed. C. A. Mace. London, 1966.

Cooke, William. *Edward Thomas: A Critical Biography.* London, 1970.

Danby, John F. "Edward Thomas," *Critical Quarterly,* 1 (Winter 1959), 308-317.

Davies, W. H. *The Complete Poems of W. H. Davies.* London, 1963.

De la Mare, Walter. *Rupert Brooke and the Intellectual Imagination.* New York, 1920.

Dickinson, G. Lowes. *J. McT. E. McTaggart.* Cambridge, 1931.

Eliot, T. S., ed. *Literary Essays of Ezra Pound.* London, 1954.

Flecker, James Elroy. *Collected Prose.* London, 1920.

Goldring, Douglas. *James Elroy Flecker.* London, 1922.

Grant, Joy. *Harold Monro and the Poetry Bookshop.* London, 1967.

Hassall, Christopher. *A Biography of Edward Marsh.* New York, 1959.

————. *Rupert Brooke.* London, 1964.

Hassall, Christopher, ed. *The Prose of Rupert Brooke.* London, 1956.

Hassall, Christopher and Denis Mathews, comps. *Eddie Marsh: Sketches for a Composite Literary Portrait of Sir Edward Marsh.* London, 1953.

Howarth, Patrick. *Squire: "Most Generous of Men."* London, 1963.

Keynes, Geoffrey, ed. *The Letters of Rupert Brooke.* London, 1968.

————. *The Poetical Works of Rupert Brooke.* London, 1946.

Keynes, J. M. *Two Memoirs.* London, 1949.

Marsh, Edward. *A Number of People.* New York, 1939.

————, ed. *Rupert Brooke: The Collected Poems.* London, 1918.

[Marsh, Edward, ed.] *Georgian Poetry: 1911-1912.* London, 1912.

————. *Georgian Poetry: 1913-1915.* London, 1915.

————. *Georgian Poetry: 1916-1917.* London, 1917.

————. *Georgian Poetry: 1918-1919.* London, 1919.

————. *Georgian Poetry: 1920-1922.* London, 1922.

Monro, Harold. *Some Contemporary Poets.* London, 1920.

Moore, G. E. *Philosophical Studies.* London, 1922.

————. *Principia Ethica.* Cambridge, 1903.

Moore, Harry T., ed. *The Collected Letters of D. H. Lawrence,* Vol. I. New York, 1962.

Paige, D. D., ed. *The Letters of Ezra Pound.* New York, 1950.

Palmer, Herbert. *Post-Victorian Poetry.* London, 1938.

Passmore, John. *A Hundred Years of Philosophy.* London, 1966.

Rogers, Timothy. *Rupert Brooke: A Reappraisal and Selection.* London, 1971.

Ross, Robert H. *The Georgian Revolt, 1910-1922: Rise and Fall of a Poetic Ideal.* Carbondale, Ill., 1965.

Russell, Bertrand. *The Autobiography of Bertrand Russell: 1872-1914.* London, 1967.

———. *My Philosophical Development.* New York, 1959.

———. *Philosophical Essays.* London, 1966.

Sassoon, Siegfried. *Siegfried's Journey: 1916-1920.* New York, 1946.

———. *The Weald of Youth.* New York, 1942.

Schilpp, Paul A., ed. *The Philosophy of Bertrand Russell.* New York, 1951.

———. *The Philosophy of G. E. Moore.* Evanston and Chicago, 1942.

Sherwood, John. *No Golden Journey: A Biography of James Elroy Flecker.* London, 1973.

Spender, Stephen. *The Making of a Poem.* London, 1955.

———. *The Struggle of the Modern.* London, 1963.

Stead, C. K. *The New Poetic.* London, 1964.

Stonesifer, Richard J. *W. H. Davies: A Critical Biography.* London, 1963.

Thomas, R. George, ed. *Letters from Edward Thomas to Gordon Bottomley.* London, 1968.

Woolf, Leonard. *Sowing: An Autobiography of the Years 1880 to 1904.* New York, 1960.

INDEX